The Real History of Dinosaurs

Mace Baker, Ph.D.

Illustrated by Joshua Suko

New Century Books
Redding, California

About the Author

Mace Baker has taught young people for over 20 years in the public school system. He earned his B.A. from Biola University, and his Ph.D. from Pacific University in Missouri. He Has been engaged in Creation Research for more than 20 years and has been conducting seminars in America, Canada, western and eastern Europe, Russia and the Philippines. He is a Research Associate for the Creation Evidence Museum in Glenrose, Texas.

About the Illustrator

Johsua Suko, his wife Kristen, and their two children, Isaiah and Rachelle currently reside in the Pacific Northwest Where Joshua works as an independent contractor in the area of computer graphics.

Contributing Artist:

Lori Jahn, pp. 106, 107
John Roberts, pp. 36, 37
Ada Vivier, pp. 38, 40, 41
Doug Wilson, pp. 59, 84, 85, 86, 91, 93, 95, 96

ISBN 978-0-9647283-1-8

First Edition Published in 1997 by New Century Books
Second Edition Published in 1998 by New Century Books
Third Edition Published in 2001 by New Century Books
Fourth Edition Published in 2007 by New Century Books

Printed and bound in the United States of America

For information on Dr. Mace Baker's lectures and seminars, the author may be contacted at: 5878 Mallard Drive, Lakeland, Florida 33809   ♦ (863) 853-5653

In literature, animals have always been popular with young people. In modern times such stories as *Lassie Come Home*, *Son of Flicka*, *National Velvet*, *Sounder* and *Old Yeller* have captured the imagination of children in a most delightful way. Stories of dogs and horses have traditionally topped the reading list of young readers. It is indeed most strange that an animal which has been extinct for perhaps thousands of years should now become a chief fascination for so many young people. Horses and dogs must now share the limelight with these great beasts of antiquity.

As late as the 1970's it was very difficult to find a dinosaur book that was of much interest to children and young people. It seems that almost overnight, the subject of dinosaurs has captivated the attention of both young people and adults in a most magnetic way. Bookstores are now filled with dinosaur books and posters. Other stores are filled with dinosaur toys and T shirts. In addition to all of this we are now able to see dinosaur programs on TV and to purchase colorful and interesting dinosaur videos.

It is indeed a very sad thing that for all of their colorfulness and interesting information, 99% of all of the dinosaur books on the public market contain at least two grievous errors which are in conflict with the observable facts of science. These two errors are herein quoted from two different dinosaur books which truly represent the 99% of the aforementioned books. First, as to the time of the dinosaurs: "The period of the earth's history in which dinosaurs lived is called the Mesozoic Era. It began 225 million years ago and ended 65 million years ago." (Helen Roney Sattler, *The New Illustrated Dinosaur Dictionary*, p. 14) Second, as to the origin of the dinosaur: "Early kinds included the thecodonts, or 'socket toothed' reptiles. From these came the crocodilians, dinosaurs, and pterosaurs (winged reptiles). " (David Lambert *The Illustrated Book of Dinosaurs*, p. 26).

Of course these ideas are antagonistic both to the revelation of our Creator as provided in the 66 books of Scripture and to the real facts of science. The Bible in general and the book of Genesis in particular represent the only valid account of the origin of the universe, of the earth, and of living things. There is certainly no indication in the books of the Bible that one animal species has evolved into another. Nor is there any such evidence in the fossil record. Another fallacy which has recently become popular is the idea that birds are the descendants of dinosaurs. "Although dinosaurs are extinct, descendants of small, insect-eating dinosaurs are still with us today. These descendants are the birds, which evolved about 150 million years ago." (George B. Johnson, *Biology Visualizing Life*, Holt, Rinehart and Winston, 1994, p. 214) [This is a California State Adopted textbook for high schools.] The French writer Pascale Chenel illustrates the internationality of this erroneous concept, "The true ancestors of birds were certainly small biped dinosaurs, not yet discovered." (Pascale Chenel, *Life and Death of Dinosaurs*, Barron's, 1987, p. 64.) The 'certainty' of Chenel's statement is certainly in conflict with the fossil evidence. As Swinton of the University of Toronto has stated, "The [evolutionary] origin of birds is largely a matter of deduction. There is no fossil evidence of the stages through which the remarkable change from reptile to bird was achieved." (W.E. Swinton, The Origin of Birds', *Biology and Comparative Physiology of Birds*, Vol. I, Academic Press, NY, 1960, p. 1) While the Biblical record is in conflict with the theory of evolution, it is not in conflict with the facts of science.

In this book I would like to provide a history of the dinosaurs which will show where they fit in earth history in a way that is compatible with both science and Scripture.

In the Book of Genesis we learn of the origin of the universe, of the earth, and of life on the earth. Genesis 1:1 states, "In the beginning God created the heaven and the earth."

ॐ *3* ॐ

From this we learn that God is the source of the material world. The world of space, time and matter is the only world of which we may obtain scientific knowledge. Of any worlds beyond this we have no knowledge except by a revelation from the Creator. Moreover, since no human was around at the time of the creation of the earth and universe, even this knowledge comes to us by courtesy of the Creator. The material or natural world from one end of the universe to another represents what in philosophical terms we call the Effect. For this great effect there must be a cause, which is superior to the effect. It is obvious that the Cause of this material universe is not just another material system. No, the cause must be greater than and different from the effect. Thus it is not at all unreasonable nor unscientific to state that a solely naturalistic explanation is inadequate to explain the origin of the natural world (earth, solar system, and universe). It is imperative that we attribute to this great effect, a super-natural cause—one that is different from and superior to the universe which we can study and experience.

Consequently, it should come as no surprise when we find on the one hand the statement from Genesis 1:1 that God created the heavens and the earth, and the statement, on the other hand, from John 4:24 that God is a Spirit. God is not the same as the universe He has created. He is transcendent to it—that is greater than and different from this material system of space, time, and matter. It is evident that He brought the universe into existence by means superior to the natural processes inherent in this universe.

The first law of Thermodynamics indicates that it was a special creation, that is to say, that it began and was completed in the past. This means that the creative processes are not observable today. This law is in full support of the creation account which indicates on the one hand that God created the earth and the universe, and on the other hand, that He finished His work of creation in a given period of time. In the book of Exodus 20:11, we read, "For in six days the Lord made heaven and earth, the sea, and all that in them is, and rested the seventh day: wherefore the Lord blessed the sabbath day, and hallowed it."

Now in Genesis 1:25 and following, we are given a record of the large groupings of physical life which the Creator brought into existence to inhabit the planet earth. It would make for a very long revelation indeed if the Creator took the time to specifically name each animal species which He created. Instead in the book of Genesis He gives us only the categories. A study of the Hebrew words shows us that all categories of animal life and plant life which we now see on the earth are accounted for in the first chapter of Genesis.

In Genesis 1:20, 21, 24, and 25 the basic kinds of animals which the Lord God created are identified. It is important to note that each of the created groups were specifically ordained and/or programmed to reproduce only their own kind. This, of course, is what we find happening in the animal world today. This is the true and unwavering experience of the biological world. Our innumerable observations show us that there are no exceptions to this phenomenon. To insinuate that there have been exceptions to this observable principle in the past is to engage in unwarranted speculation. Though such speculations have been rampant, none has ever been substantiated by any observable evidence, either in the living world or in the fossil record. Cattle never reproduce anything but cattle, monkeys never reproduce anything but monkeys, and so it is throughout the world of living creatures.

In the beginning...?

    Since 1859 the theory of evolution has become increasingly popular. In fact, it is essentially the only theory of Origins permitted in the science frameworks of the secular universities and public schools of the world. A Holt Biology text (*BIOLOGY, VISUALIZING LIFE*, 1994) for high schools states the current theory, "Most scientists think that life arose on Earth from inanimate matter, after the newly formed Earth had cooled...." (p. 199) This means that the influence of a Supernatural Creator is unnecessary for the explanation of the origin of life and for the origin of the specific kinds of plant and animal life.

However, there is no scientific evidence to support this theory. It is evident that no such changes have taken place in the natural world which we observe, nor is it possible to observe from the fossil record that such changes ever took place in the past. Carl Dunbar, a past professor at Yale University, has previously emphasized the importance of the fossil record for the theory of evolution. "Although the comparative study of living animals and plants may give very convincing circumstantial evidence, fossils provide the only historical, documentary evidence that life has evolved from simpler to more and more complex forms." (Carl O. Dunbar, *Historical Geology*, 1960, p. 47) In other words, no transitional species means no documentary evidence for evolution. The burden of proof for the theory of evolution has been placed on the paleontologist. However, Kitts states, "Evolution requires intermediate forms between species and paleontology does not provide them." (David Kitts, "Paleontology and Evolutionary Theory," *Evolution*, Vol. 128, Sept. 1974, p. 467.)

It is clear from a detailed study of biology that such vertical changes upward are not possible. Mutations are not shown to improve an organism but to subtract from the organism or to distort it. In fact, it is so obvious from the fossil record that these slow and gradual changes over long periods of time did not occur, that many modern day evolutionists have largely abandoned this particular theory of evolution, in favor of a theory that suggests that the changes were made over a much shorter period of time. The reason they suggest this is because there is no evidence from the fossil world showing that such theorized transitional types have ever existed. Thus, in order to save the theory from complete rejection by the scientific and educational community the new theory has had to be postulated. In plain words, the new theory states that since we do not find transitional types in the fossil record these transitions must have taken place in such a short time, geologically speaking, that no fossil record was laid down, preserving their fossils for our observation.

The final point to be noted in Gen 1:25 is that God states that what He had created was very good. In other words there was no need of improvement. By contrast, the whole idea of evolution is based upon the supposed need for simple species to improve until they eventually give rise to more complex species. As a 1993 Prentice Hall text for schools states, "Thus evolution means that all inhabitants of Earth are changed forms of living things that came before." (*Evolution: Change Over Time*, Prentice Hall Science, 1993, p. 48.) It is evident from the Genesis Record that no such upward transitions and no such biological improvements were needed. Genesis 1:24, 25 indicates that, from the beginning the Creator made all of the animal kinds to reproduce after their own kind so that, from the beginning, they were capable of surviving and indeed of thriving, in the environment in which the Lord God had created them.

The Genesis Record of creation indicates that God created six basic groups of animals. They are specifically listed in Genesis 1:20-25. First, we have the "beast of the earth." The Hebrew word is *chayah eretz*. Some of these Hebrew words appear to have both a broader meaning and a narrow meaning. For instance, *chayah eretz* appears, at times, to apply to all of the animals God created. Yet on occasion, it may refer primarily to wild and/or carnivorous animals.

Second, we have the "cattle." The Hebrew word, *behema*, appears to refer not merely to cattle, but to all of the animals which man has found easy to domesticate. This would include goats, horses, camels, donkeys, sheep, etc. Cattle, of course, are plant eating animals which man has been able to use for meat, milk, hide and, in the case of oxen, as beasts of burden. These uses are in general applicable to a number of other animals which God created. In Exodus 9:3 we read, "Behold, the hand of the Lord is upon thy cattle which is in the field, upon the horses, upon the asses, upon the camels, upon the oxen, and upon the sheep...." In Joshua 8:2 we read, "And thou shalt do to Ai and her king as thou didst unto Jericho and her king: only the spoil thereof, and the cattle thereof, shall ye take for a prey unto yourselves...." It is unlikely that the victors would take the cattle specifically, while leaving behind large flocks of sheep and large quantities of goats or camels. In those days all of these animals were very valuable. It is most probable that *behema* carried the same connotation then as does our own word "livestock" today.

Third, we have "the creeping things." The Hebrew word is *remes*. *Remes* appears to refer to all of the animals which do not have the normal appendages for locomotion, like those of the mammals and the reptiles. This category includes such creatures as worms, insects, spiders, etc. In Psalm 104:25 it is apparent that *remes* also includes crabs, lobsters, etc. "So is this great and wide sea, wherein are things creeping innumerable...."

Fourth, we have the "fish of the sea." The Hebrew word *degat-hayom* appears to refer to all of the marine animals in the sea and oceans, except for such as the sea anemones and invertebrates and the like. The difference in these kinds is expressed in Habakkuk 1:14 which reads, "And makest men as the fishes of the sea, as the creeping things, that have no ruler over them?"

Fifth, we have the "fowl of the air." Here the Hebrew word *oph hashamayim* refers to all animals which have wings, and probably to all flightless birds as well. These are mentioned with a variety of other animals in Psalms 148:10, "Beasts, and all cattle; creeping things, and flying fowl."

Now as we review all of the animals which we see on the earth today, we find that they all fit very comfortably within these five specific categories. Yet, oddly enough, the Scriptures list six categories. Since all of our animals today fit within the five previously listed categories, to what could the sixth category of animal refer? The Hebrew word is *tannim*. This word occurs in the Old Testament about 25 times. Whatever animal is meant by the word *tannim*, was obviously alive from the time of Genesis to the time of Malachi, since it was mentioned in both of those books. The word actually refers to an animal that is now extinct. That is why it has been challenging for some Bible commentaries to properly identify these creatures.

Most of the time in the King James Version, it is properly translated by the English word "dragon." Such as in Isaiah 43:20 where we read, "The beast of the field shall honor me, the dragons and the owls...."

Draco

The KJV translators are to be congratulated for their choice of word in this translation. It is always a challenge to figure out what animal is meant by a certain Hebrew word. In this case, the KJV translators chose the English word "dragon."

Why, we may ask, did they choose that word? These scholars knew ancient history as well as some of the more important languages of ancient history. They chose the word "dragon" which actually comes to us from the Greek word "draco." And what does "draco" mean? It has a very specific meaning.

There were actually several different languages spoken by the ancient Greeks. Alexander the Great saw the need to merge the languages into one common Greek language. That has become known as "koine" or common Greek. It is, of course, the language in which the New Testament is written.

Prior to 1842 the various members of the class Reptilia were organized into four separate orders. The first order was that of the serpents, the second of that was the alligators/crocodiles, the third was that of the turtles, and the fourth was that of the lizards. Doubtless, the scientists of ancient Greece would have organized the reptiles into similar categories.

Now, it is important to note that "draco" does not mean serpent, turtle, alligator or lizard. It means a reptilian-like being. The serpents, of course, have no appendages, but move across the earth flat on their stomachs. All of the other members of the reptiles, however, move with what is called a sprawling gait. Their arms and legs are more or less splayed out to the side, whereas the mammals, such as bears, lions, and zebras have their legs straight under them. The ancient Greeks noticed that these unique creatures looked reptilian, yet did not walk with a normal reptilian gait, instead it was observed that they held their legs straight under them, as did the mammals. This must have been very puzzling to the ancient Greek people who would see them from time to time. Consequently, they identified them with the word "draco." In a word, they were saying, "these are reptiles of a most unusual kind."

Genesis 1:21 actually says, "And God created great *tannim*...." It seems apparent that whatever is mentioned here includes among its number some animals of "great" size. In most cases the KJV scholars properly translated "*tannim*" by the word "*dragon*." However, in Genesis 1:21 they used the word "whale." It is probable that they chose the word "whale" because the animal in this verse is next to a Hebrew phrase which talks about the creation of marine life. "And God created great whales, and every living creature that moveth, which the waters brought forth abundantly...." Further, the animal mentioned here is said to be "great." It is possible that the scholars associated the word "great" with sea life and consequently came up with the word "whale." However, it is to be noted that there are three distinct categories of animal mentioned in Genesis 1:21: *tannim*, *degat-hayom*, and *oph hashamayim*. As we know, whales are very much marine animals and it is unlikely that they would occupy a category by themselves. As we will soon see, this is not the case.

It is further to be noted that two of the animals mentioned in this verse (fish and fowl) both bring their young into the world by means of eggs. By contrast, whales bring their young into the world live, as do humans. Perhaps there is a hint in this verse, then, that the animal in question is also one that brings their young into the world by means of eggs.

As we study this particular Hebrew word, "tannin", in its varied use throughout Scripture it becomes evident that the use of the English word "whale" in Genesis 1:21 was a mistake. This fact can be graphically illustrated by observing two separate passages in the Book of Exodus. In the fourth chapter of Exodus we find Moses with his rod. God is about to show Moses His own power by means of Moses' rod. When Moses cast it on the ground it became a living animal. In the KJV we read, "And the Lord said unto him, What is that in thine hand? And he said, A rod. And he said, Cast it on the ground. And he cast it on the ground, and it became a serpent..." (Exodus 4:2,3). The word translated here as "serpent" is the Hebrew word, "nahash." "Nahash" is also found in such passages as Genesis 3:1 "the serpent was more subtle than any beast of the field", Proverbs 23:32 "it biteth like a serpent", Job 26:13 "his hand has formed the crooked serpent", Isaiah 27:1 "even leviathan that crooked serpent" and Micah 7:17 "lick the dust like a serpent".

Now by contrast we find that Aaron also had a rod and Aaron also cast it to the ground. When he did so it became a living animal. In Exodus 7:10 we read, "...And Aaron cast down his rod before Pharaoh...and it became a serpent." However, in this case the Hebrew word used is not, as would be expected, "nahash" but "tannin." Obviously, Moses' rod and the rod of Aaron were not changed into the same kind of animal. If we insist that the translation in Genesis 1:21 is correct then we are obligated here to translate the word "tannim" as "whale." We understand, of course, that if the rod had been changed into a whale that it would have certainly obtained Pharaoh's attention, but it does indeed seem unlikely that this was actually the case.

It is of value to recall that Jesus in Matthew 12:40 spoke of Jonah in the belly of the whale. The Greek word used here is "ketos." Liddel and Scott in their Greek-English Lexicon say that "ketos" refers to a sea monster or any huge fish (p. 949-950). Now we know that Jesus was referring to the original reference to this incident as recorded in the ancient book of Jonah. Consequently, Jesus and the prophet Jonah are both referring to the same aquatic animal. What then does Jonah's text say? The first reference occurs in Jonah 1:17, "Now the Lord had prepared a great fish to swallow up Jonah. And Jonah was in the belly of the fish three days and three nights." The Hebrew word used here for fish is "dag." The same word is found in Jonah 2:1 and 10. This is the normal word used throughout the Old Testament for fish. Now, if in Jonah's account we would have found that the Hebrew word translated into the English as huge fish would have been *tannim* rather than *dag*, then the translation in Genesis 1:21 of *tannim* as whales would be more reasonable. However, we find in the very instance where a whale or whale like creature is named the word is not *tannim* but *dag*. Thus, we must conclude that the translation of *tannim* as "whales" is erroneous.

It seems most logical, therefore, in keeping with the original language, to believe that the rod of Moses became one kind of animal and the rod of Aaron became another. As mentioned before, the vast majority of time the word "tannin" is properly translated "dragon." So, also here in the case of Aaron's rod, it would seem best that the word "tannin" be translated "dragon." In both cases, then the rods would have been turned into reptiles. Despite the popularity of the great *Brontosaurus* and his kind in today's press, most of the dinosaurs were of much smaller stature. Thus, it is quite reasonable from a biological standpoint to assume that the one rod became a serpent and that the second rod became a reptile of a different sort—a dragon.

In Genesis 1:21, the use of the plural *tannim* is significant since we know from the fossil evidence that there were many kinds of dinosaurs. In fact, it is conservatively suggested by the experts that about 335 species have now been discovered. Although, historically, dinosaur paleontologists have had a rather liberal attitude with regard to the "creation" of new species, it is evident that there were nevertheless many kinds of these creatures in the past.

Now in Genesis 1:31 we read, "And God saw everything that He had made, and, behold, it was very good." Again, the point must be made that from the beginning the Creator so created every living kind that they were perfectly suited to the environment into which they were placed. There was no need for further improvement and no animal was in any way deficient. In a word, evolution was not necessary. Further, it would appear quite contrary to the nature of God that He, the One who by definition is all-knowing and all-powerful, should have to first create a primitive species of animals and then have to wait for millions of years before they finally, through the clumsy process of mutations and natural selection, reach greater and greater categories of improvement. Today, the manufacturers only put the products on the market when they are ready to do the work advertised. So also God, who brought everything into existence through His spoken word and by his divine power, would not likely bring into existence a host of biological beings, which due to the various problems encountered in their environment, would have immediately been in peril. Horizontal change, due to expected changes in the environment, would have been already programmed into the organism. Thus, over time we could get (as we do have today) many varieties of flying squirrels. However, they are all flying squirrels. None are half mouse or weasel, nor are any in the process of changing.

The Genesis Record tells us that God's work of creation lasted only six days. In that amount of time the universe, the plant world, the animals and the first two human beings were created. Following this we learn of the great temptation which ended in what has come to be known as the "Fall" of man. The Fall, of course, refers to the severance of man's life-sustaining relationship with the Creator. The spiritual bond was broken. At that time man obtained a nature which has the capacity and willingness to do both good and evil. Hence in our own time and throughout history we see men and women doing many good works even works of charity. However, we also see mankind continually engaged in a great variety of unrighteous behaviorisms. In fact, in each of our own lives we can clearly see that doing right consistently is no easy task. We are so frequently tempted to behave in a way that is at variance even with our own conscience. By and by, of course, man has developed the habit of redefining what the path of righteousness is. The net effect of this has been for man to develop a "relative" righteousness. It is acceptable to him as he views himself, but it is not acceptable to God. One of the purposes of the written revelation of God is to show us the vast difference between the righteousness of man and that of God.

We learn from the book of Genesis that as time went by the transgression of man increased. We further learn that the deviation which the revelation of God calls "sin" spread throughout the world and became increasingly intense. The apparent history of man's deviation from God is first illustrated in the case of Cain, the first child of Adam and Eve. He was provided with more than adequate knowledge of God and of His plan for man's redemption. Nevertheless, though he was forced to acknowledge the reality and power of God, he did not acknowledge the necessity for a redeemer. In time the descendants of Cain, as well as many of the descendants of Abel, left off even the acknowledgement of the deity and power of the Creator. In turning from Him they turned from the influence of His righteous character. This left them with no other guide to right living but that only of their own fallen nature.

The nature of the problem is recorded for us in the early chapters of Genesis. In Genesis 6:5 we read, "And God saw that the wickedness of man was great in the earth, and that every imagination of the thoughts of his heart was only evil continually." The phrase, "only evil continually" describes the low level of moral decadence to which man had descended. Again, in Genesis 6:11 we are told, "The earth also was corrupt before God, and the earth was filled with violence." Then, as in our own day, the increase of sin or wickedness resulted in a marked increase of violence. It was quite apparent that the future of the human race hung in the balance.

It seems apparent that God foresaw that, unless radical steps were taken, the entire human race would have been destroyed by means of its own wickedness. The physical destruction of the human race or the elimination of all "true believers" would have essentially served the same purpose. It would have made the promise of redemption as prophesied in the early chapters of Genesis, impossible to fulfill. God's original purpose for mankind would have been completely thwarted. The intensity of the problem according to the divine evaluation demanded strong and powerful action on the part of the Creator.

The corrective action that God chose to take is recorded in Genesis 6:17, "And, I, even I, do bring a flood of waters upon the earth, to destroy all flesh, wherein is the breath of life, from under heaven; and every thing that is in the earth shall die." The radical remedy which God applied to the problems may seem harsh to us, but according to the all-wise God it was the necessary step to take in order to insure that mankind would not only have a future, but a future in which the goodness and mercy and grace of God would be eternally influential.

God's plan for preserving the human race called for a great judgment and a new start for mankind. According to the Genesis account, the population of mankind had so completely involved themselves in unbelief and wicked behavior that there was at the time of the judgment only one family left who worshipped the Lord God and practiced the principles of right living. Only Noah and his family believed in the Lord God as Creator and respected the promise of a coming Redeemer. By the time of the great judgment no other family was worshiping the Lord God. Neither were they obedient to His principles of righteousness.

Consequently, God informed Noah of the impending judgment and instructed him to take precautionary measures for the protection of himself, his family and of representative species of the animal world. Noah's primary responsibility in lieu of the coming judgment was the building of an ark (a large cargo barge) which would be able to carry him, his family and representative species of the animal world, through the peril of the coming judgment. In Genesis 6:14 we read of God's instructions, "Make thee an ark of gopher wood; rooms shalt thou make in the ark, and shalt pitch it within and without with pitch."

The particular kind of craft which the Lord God designed is of significant importance. We have a variety of accounts of such a vessel from various cultures. The Hebrew account however, is the only one that gives any precise measurements or that gives precise measurements that would make a vessel sea worthy. The Genesis Record gives the measurements in terms of a cubit. From ancient literature we learn that there was more than one kind of cubit. One was a longer cubit and one was a shorter cubit. Even if we take the shortest cubit however, we find that the ark was a most imposing vessel. If built today it would measure 437 feet in length, about 72 feet in width and about 43 feet in depth. It would have the volume of about 1,396,000 cu. ft. It could carry about as much as 522 railroad stock cars. This means that the ark could carry more than 125,000 sheep size animals.

It is important to note in this section that God, the Creator of the living world, goes on record that it is He who will destroy it, and that He will destroy it with a great flood of waters. "And behold, I, even I, do bring a flood of waters upon the earth, to destroy all flesh, wherein is the breath of life, from under heaven; and everything that is in the earth shall die." (Genesis 6:17) A number of important points are made within this long sentence. 1) God is the One who is responsible for the judgment. 2) The judgment is going to be by a global flood. This would of course mean that living things will be drowned and many of them will inevitably become buried in the eroded material. 3) The purpose is to destroy all flesh. To this there is one qualifier—all flesh "wherein is the breath of life." This means that the judgment is not essentially against the creatures of the oceans and the seas. This also means that Noah was not required to develop some kind of an aquarium aboard the ark for sea life. 4) Apart from the ocean, sea and fresh water organisms, everything that was on the earth was to die. There were to be no exceptions. To say any other creature escaped by swimming is to disregard both the express Word of God and the power of God in this matter.

Finally after many years and much work, Noah and his sons finished building the ark. God then influenced the representative species of all the animals to go aboard the ark, after which Noah and his family, following God's instructions, went aboard.

The Scriptures are very clear that Noah was to take two of each kind of air breathing species aboard the ark (and seven of each "clean" kind). However, in modern times, many people have probably challenged this statement since they have found from the fossil record that some of the land dwelling creatures-- dinosaurs--became so very large. How could Noah have gotten a 30 ton *Apatosaurus* or a 90 foot *Diplodocus* aboard the ark?

Thankfully, the fossil evidence shows us very clearly that this was indeed not a difficult problem. "Since 1859, dinosaur eggs and eggshells, as well as baby dinosaurs, have been found on almost every continent...." (Kenneth Carpenter, Karl F. Hirsch, and John R. Horner, *Dinosaur Eggs and Babies*, p. 2). The largest are about the size of cannonballs. Thus, we see that dinosaurs despite their great size as adult specimens, started life in a very small package.

Many young dinosaurs have been found and we can, in the case of some families, trace their growth stages from nest to adult. Consider this report, "Trackways found this year in South Korea show the marks of scores of tiny, milling brontosaurs, the size of calves." (Sharon Begley and Emily Yoffee, "New Theories and Old Bones Reveal the Lifestyles of the Dinosaur" *Newsweek*, October 28, 1991, p. 53.) An adult, *Brontosaurus* (now known as *Apatosaurus*) was about 70 feet long and weighed about 35 tons. In South Korea, however, we find that the young brontosaurs were only the size of calves. It is obvious then that God would have ordered the younger dinosaurs aboard the ark for at least two good reasons. The first is that younger sauropods would have taken up less room. The second is that after the Flood the dinosaurs like all of the other animals were obligated to multiply and fill the earth. Younger dinosaurs rather than older members of a given species would have been much more sexually virile and thus would have been more able to fulfill God's command.

So, we can be sure that all of the air breathing mammal species and all of the air breathing reptilian species (that were not oriented to an aquatic *modus operandi*, such as the ichthyosaurs) would have been taken aboard the ark. Even birds would have had to be taken aboard the ark. It is unreasonable to believe that any bird could have survived the long duration of the Flood or the extremely dangerous atmospheric conditions which prevailed for such a long period of time. This of course is why we find many bird fossils in the sedimentary strata. They, like many of the other air breathing species, eventually drowned in the rising waters, and many of those that drowned were also buried by the eroded sediments.

If the Flood had been a local one, no cargo vessel of this size would have been needed. Furthermore, if it was to have been merely a local Flood, then Noah could have been instructed to take his family and journey to a far country where for the time being they could be safe. Later on in Biblical history, the patriarch Jacob, when there was a famine in the land, took his family to Egypt. An ark of this size and of this excellent design was definitely made for the purpose of a great, indeed global and prolonged Flood. Many ancient historical accounts have been written which testify to the actuality of a global Flood.

The ancient Egyptian account is unique in that it states that the Flood occurred on the same day as that documented in Genesis. "With the Deluge tradition the Egyptians connected the commemoration of the dead....This ceremony was observed on the 17th day of Athyr, which corresponds to the date found in the Mosaic account of the Flood." (John Urquhart, *Modern Discoveries and the Bible*, p. 175).

The Genesis record indicates that the global Flood had two specific sources: the breaking up of the "fountains of the great deep" and the opening up of the "windows of heaven." The latter source resulted in rain pouring upon the earth for "forty days and forty nights." (Gen. 7: 11, 12). The geological record demonstrates that the breaking up of the "fountains of the deep" was in fact the more or less simultaneous eruption of a very large number of volcanoes throughout a vast region of the ocean floor. "By any standard, the outpouring of volcanic rock in the southwestern Pacific in late Mesozoic and early Cenozoic time was incomparably the greatest in the geological record." (H.W. Menard, *Marine Geology of the Pacific*, McGraw-Hill Bk. Co.,1964, p. 95). The term "Mesozoic" refers to one of the evolutionary time zones -- the one in which the dinosaurs lived. The observable evidence is simply that these are flood sediments which contain dinosaur fossils. The evidence in the rocks does not support a slow and gradual (over millions of years) development. However, the evidence does show that during the same era in which dinosaurs were being drowned, buried, and fossilized, enormous volcanic activity was also taking place upon the ocean floor.

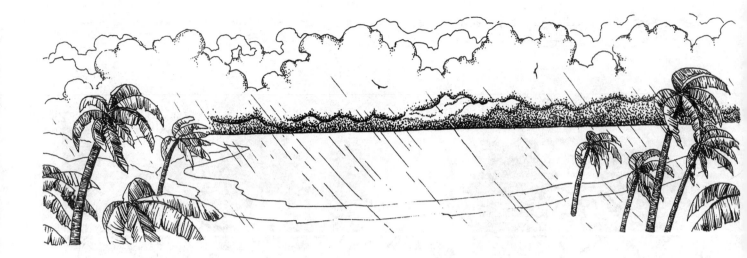

Then, the Scriptures say that after forty days and forty nights the rains discontinued. Apparently, the rains were for the purpose of developing flooding inland, long before the ocean waters covered the continent. By means of these two sources of water (the ocean and the rains) the whole earth could be covered in the times stated in Genesis—about 6 to 8 months. Actually, the total duration of the Flood was 371 days. If only ocean waters (and/or fountains of the deep) would have been used, it seems apparent that the Flood would have taken much longer. This would have made it much more difficult for those aboard the ark. (The longer the amount of time within the ark, the greater amount of food storage space would be needed.) The two flood sources were great enough to ensure coverage of the whole earth, while being rapid enough to keep the time spent aboard the ark to a minimum.

The opening of the "windows of heaven" resulted in the elimination of the vast canopy of water which had from the beginning surrounded the earth. One of the main benefits of this protective water canopy was to shield both man and animals from harmful solar radiation. The canopy is in part what contributed to the extraordinarily long human life spans as recorded in the book of Genesis. It is likely that even the animals of the antediluvian world also lived longer in those days. One of the most noticeable effects of the loss of this great vapor canopy is to be seen in the increasingly shorter and shorter life spans of man after the Flood. It seems apparent that God preferred that the human beings who lived after the Flood should have shorter life spans. This doubtless had the effect of retarding the growth of evil and wickedness in the new world.

Climate and weather conditions were also greatly effected by the loss of the vapor canopy. In the antediluvian world the earth enjoyed mild to sub-tropical climate on a global scale. In our present world, variations of climate and severe weather conditions make life much more challenging and difficult than it was before the great Flood.

Eventually, the flood waters covered all of the mountains and hills so that all land surfaces were now under water. The next step in God's program was then to remove this massive quantity of water that now covered the earth. This was achieved by two means: by the raising up of high mountain ranges and by the development of deep ocean basins. These actions are referred to in Psalm 104:6-8 (NASV). "The waters were standing above the mountains. At thy rebuke they fled; At the sound of Thy thunder they hurried away. The mountains rose; the valleys [basins] sank down to the place which Thou didst establish for them."

The statement with regard to the rising of the mountains is supported by our observation that the Earth's great mountain ranges are uplifted mountains composed largely of igneous rock, but often covered with sedimentary rocks. The great Flood eroded, transported and deposited material in layers all over the earth. Then, during the latter half of the Flood, the mountain building process began, causing these newly developed mountain ranges to rise higher and higher. The sedimentary layers of these uplifted mountains contain fossils...the remains of animals that were buried during the first half of the Flood year. Further, these mountain ranges are considered by geologists to be young, that is to say of recent origin in earth history.

With regard to the Himalayas, we read, "As you walk in the Himalayas, and if you have been taught to look for it, you can find evidence of these cataclysmic events. The first is the presence of fossilized sea-animals high up on the slopes....These ammonites have been found in the Himalayas as high as 18,000 feet. The uppermost levels are limestone, a rock formed by the gradual deposit on the seabed of the shells of marine creatures. There can be only one explanation: as the continents collided and reared upwards at their edges, part of the original seabed between them was carried up with the deeper rocks." (Nickolson, Nigel: *The Himalayas* - Time Life Books, p. 26)

The evidence shows that the phenomenon of mountain building was both recent and global. For instance, such recent mountain building is recognized in North America, in Europe, in central Asia, and in South America. "In addition to these tectonic movements many of the high volcanic cones around the Pacific border, in western and central Asia and in eastern Africa, are believed to have been built up to their present great heights during the Pliocene and Pleistocene." (R.F. Flint, *Glacial Geology and the Pleistocene Epoch,* New York, Wiley, 1947, pp. 514-15) In the evolutionary scenario, late Tertiary, Pliocene, and Pleistocene represent very recent geological eras. Further, as Whitcomb and Morris conclude, "...and since nearly all of the great mountain areas of the world have been found to have fossils from these times near their summits, there is no conclusion possible other than that the mountains ... have all been uplifted essentially simultaneously and quite recently." (John C. Whitcomb, Jr. and Henry Morris, *The Genesis Flood*, Baker Book House, 1961, p.128)

The statement in Psalm 104, regarding the sinking down of the basins, refers to the phenomenon which geologists now identify as "subsidence." The vast floor of the Pacific Ocean now contains a large number of submerged volcanic mountains known as sea mounts. These volcanic mountains which erupted at the beginning of the Flood year represent the original "fountains of the great deep." At that time the ocean was relatively shallow. However, they are now found at significant depths on the ocean floor. The most reasonable explanation for the present position of these many volcanic mountains which litter the floor of the Pacific, is that in the past they sank beneath the ocean waters. "In summary, a hypothesis of elevation and subsidence of a broad region of the southwestern Pacific most satisfactorily accounts for the sinking of almost all guyots and atolls." (H. W. Menard *op. cit.* p. 95)

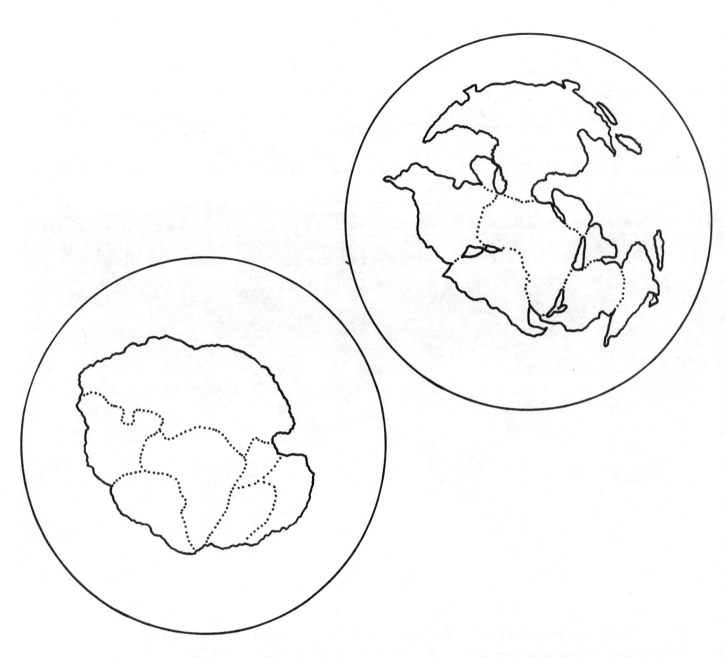

Among the many geological results of the great global Flood was the radical tectonic activity that initiated the splitting of the single continent into a variety of smaller land masses. "The fit of South America and Africa, ancient climatic similarities, fossil evidence, and rock structures all seemed to support the idea that these now-separate land masses were once joined." (Frederick K. Lutgens and Edward J. Tarbuck, *Essentials of Geology*, Merrill Publishing Company, 1989, p. 257). The evolutionary geology textbooks portray this event as having taken place during the Mesozoic era. Their maps show "continental drift" as beginning during the Triassic, continuing through the Jurassic and completing during the Cretaceous period. This idea theorizes a time span of approximately 155 million years.

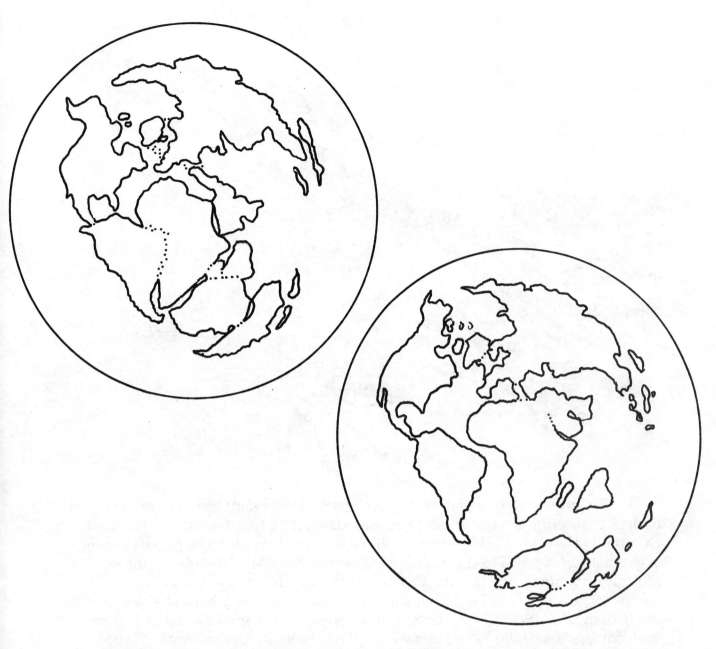

The book of Genesis, however, seems to indicate that this event probably began during the last half of the Flood year and culminated a few hundred years later during the lifetime of Peleg. "And unto Eber were born two sons: the name of one was Peleg; for in his days was the earth divided..." (Gen. 10:25) This period of time included at least four generations: those of Arphaxad, Salah, Eber and Peleg. Though this time gap differs greatly from the evolutionary scenario, it does, nevertheless, provide an adequate amount of time for the animals to have migrated so that when the separation became extensive they would have already found suitable environments on all the major land areas.

Though the master continent broke apart, it is evident that a variety of land bridges connecting the larger land masses existed for a long time after the Flood. Eventually these land bridges were reduced in area, possibly in large part because of the melting of post-Flood glaciers. Dinosaurologist, Dale Russel, writing of geological events during the late Cretacious (evolutionary time zonation), acknowledges that, "...a land-bridge linked Labrador and southern Greenland with the British Isles. South of the bridge, at its broadest, the growing Atlantic Ocean was still less than 1500 kilometers wide." (Dale Russell, *An Odyssey in Time, Dinosaurs of North America*, NorthWord Press, 1989 p. 94)

Even today, remnants of the ancient land bridges are still obvious, as in the case of the Aleutian Islands. In the past, these islands were part of a much more prominent strip of land. Professor Charles Hapgood, reporting on a map compiled by Turkish cartographer Hadji Ahmed (1559 A.D.), talks of a land bridge connecting Alaska and Siberia, "This land bridge actually existed in the so-called Ice Age. The map suggests that the land bridge was a broad one, perhaps a thousand miles across." (Charles Hapgood, *Maps of the Ancient Sea Kings*, Chilton Books, Philadelphia and New York, 1966, p. 98.)

The rebellion against the Lord God which occurred prior to the Flood was renewed almost immediately in the new population that developed after the Flood. This rebellion culminated in the building of the Tower of Babel. The Tower of Babel incident is of great importance, not only because it represents a wicked attempt to unite the populace under one centralized government, but also because it marks the beginning of human languages. It was God's purpose for the descendants of Noah, in their various families, to spread out, colonize the entire earth, and to govern these many and varied areas by means of local governments. However, under the evil leadership of Nimrod, an attempt was made to develop a strong central government which would, "…soon be able to produce a self-sufficient civilization capable of…controlling the entire world." (Henry Morris, *The Genesis Record*, Baker Book House, 1976 p. 268) The divine work of creating languages totally frustrated this scheme. The birth of new languages resulted in the development of thousands of new vocabularies. Examples of this, with regard to our study, can be seen in the variety of words used to identify the dinosaur. The English word "dinosaur" comes from two Greek words, "dino" and "sauria", which means "terrible lizard." The word "dragon", which is found in the King James version of the Bible, as well as in other literature, was taken from the Greek word "draco", which means "a reptilian-like being." However, the Chinese word for the same animal is "Konglong," which means "terrible dragon." The Hebrew word for both the land dragons (dinosaurs) and the sea dragons is "tannim".

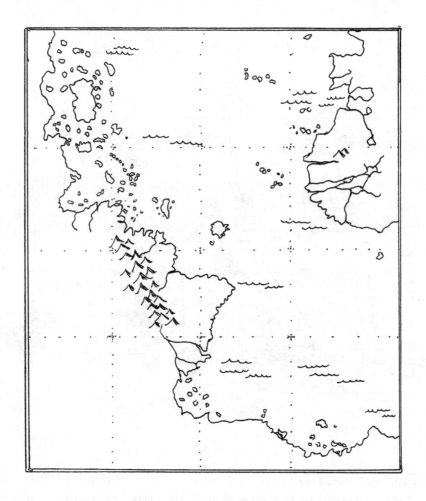

The giant tectonic forces involved in the global Flood resulted in the splitting
apart of the master continent. This led to the creation of the Atlantic Ocean and to
the movement of large chunks of Pangea such as Australia and Antarctica to
locations quite distant from the master continent. The fossil remains found in
Antarctica confirm the fact that this land was once located much farther north and
once enjoyed a mild to subtropical climate. The drifting apart of the continents has
been pictured for us by ancient cartographers. Their work, done over probably
several hundred years time, shows the changes that occurred in Antarctica as the
new climate conditions began to develop and as Antarctica drifted closer and closer
to the south pole. In the course of history, three maps were made by ancient
cartographers who began to explore the earth in the first thousand years after the
Flood. The earliest of these cartographers' maps of Antarctica was discovered and
passed on to us by Philippe Buache, the eighteenth-century French geographer.
This map appears to show Antarctica at a time when it was entirely devoid of ice.
(Charles Hapgood, *Maps of the Ancient Sea Kings*, Chilton Books, Philadelphia and
New York, 1966, p. 93) This would obviously have been during the first few
hundred years after the Tower of Babel dispersion. The next map (above,
simplified) was collected by Piri Reis, an Admiral of the Navy during the time of the
Ottoman Turks.

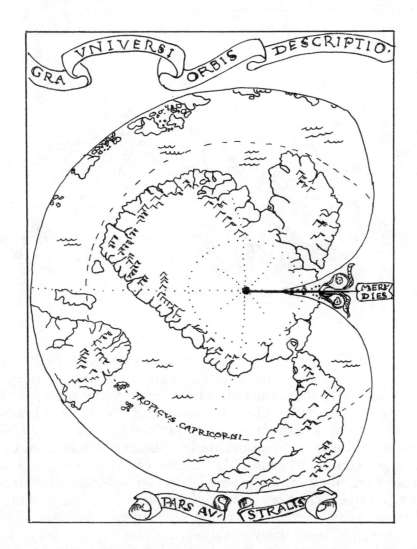

GRA VNIVERSI ORBIS DESCRIPTIO.

MERI DIES

TROPICVS CAPRICORNI

PARS AV STRALIS

This map, made at Constantinople in A.D. 1513, shows that at this time the northern coast of Antarctica was free of ice. In addition to this, we have the map discovered by Oronteus Finaeus (above, simplified) which also shows Antarctica to have mountains, rivers, and ice-free coasts. "...Fjord-like estuaries are seen, along with broad inlets and indications of rivers of a magnitude that is consistent with the sizes of the present glaciers. And some of these fjords are located remarkably close to the current position of the glaciers..." (Ibid.) Finally, in more recent times, we have the map prepared by Gerard Kremer (popularly known as Mercator). This map shows Antarctica's mountains and rivers entirely covered with ice. How was it possible that Piri Reis, Oronteus Finaeus and Philippe Buache were able to obtain such maps? Charles Hapgood, who first reported these maps, reasons as follows: "It appears that the charts must have originated with a people unknown and they were passed on, perhaps by the Minoans and the Phoenicians, who were, for a thousand years and more, the greatest sailors of the ancient world. We have evidence that they were collected and studied in the great library of Alexandria (Egypt) and the compilations of them were made by the geographers who worked there." (Ibid, revised edition, preface, 1979.)

As a result of the Tower of Babel incident, separation of the first post-Flood civilization was now inevitable. This resulted in an immediate geographic expansion by the many different families. The strongest and most intelligent families (which soon became tribes) took possession of the choicest lands in and around Mesopotamia. The weaker tribes were pushed further away from these great centers and eventually into distant lands. "As a tribe migrated to an unexplored region, it would find a suitable location (most commonly on a high elevation for protection, but near a spring or river, with fertile alluvial plains, for water and food supply) and then try to establish a village. Although members of the tribe certainly knew many useful arts, such as agriculture, animal husbandry, ceramics, metallurgy, and so on, they could not use them right away. Veins of metal had to be discovered, mined, and smeltered; suitable clay mud had to be found for making bricks and pottery; animals had to be bred; and crops had to be planted. All of this might take several years. In the meantime, the tribe had to survive by hunting, fishing, and gathering fruits and nuts. Temporary homes had to be built of stone, if available, or timber, or even in caves." (Morris, *op cit.*, p. 275)

The "cave man" has been used extensively by the evolutionary establishment to convince the public that our ancestors were ignorant, brutish sub-humans, who lived in caves and went around with a big club, often times dragging their women behind them. This distorted concept is not supported by any anthropological evidence. On the contrary, when we do find caves in which ancient people had at least temporarily resided, we find art work that is far too sophisticated to be attributed to sub-humans.

Cases in point, for instance are to be found in France and Spain. "The low ceiling of the so-called Hall of Bulls at Lascaux (fig. 1-7) is covered with bulls and horses, often partly superimposed, painted with such vitality that they fairly thunder off the rock surfaces at us." (H.W. Janson, *History of Art,* Vol. I, 1995, Prentice-Hall, p.41)

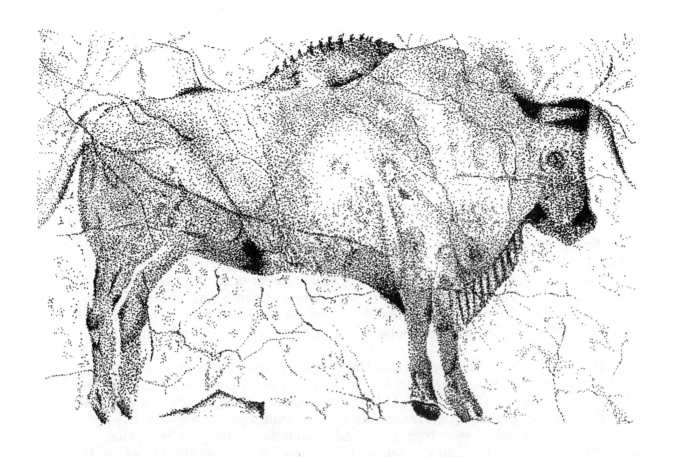

In the Altamira caves near Santander, Spain, one can view, "The great bison...painted on the ceiling of a long, narrow corridor leading from a subterranean cave in Altamira. It does not stand alone. A whole herd surges majestically across the roof, one animal overlapping another—horses, boars, mammoths, and other creatures, all the desired quarry of the Stone Age huntsman." (Sister Wendy Beckett, *Sister Wendy's Story of Painting*, D.K. Publishing Books, 1994, p.10)

One of the world's greatest archaeologists of the past, William F. Albright, comments on man's early art as follows, "...though the number of motifs, techniques and media available to him now is, of course, immeasurably greater, it is very doubtful whether man's artistic capabilities are actually any higher today than they were in late prehistoric times." (William F. Albright, *From The Stone Age to Christianity*, Doubleday Anchor, 1957, p. 165)

Prehistorian Robert Silverberg says, "The cave paintings are upsetting to those who prefer to think of Quaternary man as little more than an ape. Not only do they indicate great craftsmanship, but they point to a whole constellation of conclusions: That primitive man had an organized society with continuity and shape, religion and art. It was also dismaying to learn that the earliest inhabitants of Western Europe...had scaled heights of artistic achievement that would not be reached again until late in the Christian era." (Robert Silverberg, *Man Before Adam*, Philadelphia: Macrae Smith Co., 1964, p. 191)

As the young civilizations began to grow the advanced skills of these early peoples were soon expressed not only in the matters of agriculture and animal husbandry, but also in their art and ability to construct large buildings of stone. We have seen the marvelous works of art in the caves of France and Spain. Their masterful abilities to move and utilize great stones can been seen in many parts of the world including England (Stonehenge) and Egypt (the great pyramids.)

Soon also, as we have seen from the various maps of Antarctica, a great new age of exploration began. However, the explorers found this new world to be much different than the one that Noah and his sons had inhabited. For one thing, they found that there were now vast mountain ranges, and that, in general, the mountains were much higher than they had been before. Judging from the paleontological and geological evidence, Colbert says regarding the terrain of the ancient world (the world of the times of the dinosaurs), "Lands generally were low with no great elevations above sea level. There were hills but probably no great mountain ranges to act as barriers to the circulation of moisture-laden winds..." (Edwin H. Colbert, *Dinosaurs, An Illustrated History,* Hammond Incorporated. 1986 p. 198). Most of these great mountains with which we are now familiar are the direct result of Noah's Flood.

In their travels, the early explorers would also have found vast quantities of sedimentary rocks which had been developed by the global Flood. In these, they would have often seen multiple layers consisting of mudstone, sandstone and siltstone. In some locations, they would have also found various thicknesses of coal seams interbedded between layers of mudstone or sandstone. These coal seams would have represented the vast quantity of plants which had existed in the world before the Flood, when the weather and atmospheric conditions were conducive to the rich growth of vegetation.

Besides finding geological evidences of the great Flood such as the vast sedimentary layers, they also found geological evidences of the great run-off. In many parts of the world the flood waters returning to the ocean had eroded great quantities of rock and left behind hills and mounds and mountains made up primarily of horizontally laid sedimentary layers of rocks. In some areas such as Bryce Canyon in Utah, hundreds of pinnacles of stone were left behind as the flood waters ran off across the area of southwestern USA.

By and by as these people and their descendants crossed over various outcroppings of sedimentary rocks they came upon large quantities of fossilized bones. These were the bones of the animals that had perished during the great flood. Many of the animals simply drowned and floated for a long time in the water. After awhile they settled to the bottom. When the waters left the earth, the bones were exposed to oxygen, and they soon became oxidized and rotted away back into the soil. Many of the creatures which died in the Flood, however, were buried by the great quantities of sediments which the flood waters had eroded and transported across the continent. Their numerous bones tell us a most graphic story of the great judgment which God brought upon the earth during the time of Noah.

In many cases, they found huge graveyards filled with thousands of fossilized bones. The more the descendants of Noah spread out upon the earth, the more places fossils were found. In some layers the bones were primarily fish or various forms of marine life; in other formations, primarily dinosaurs and other reptiles, while in others primarily mammals. In the case of the dinosaurs for instance, there are many huge mass burial sites. The site at Como Bluffs, Wyoming, was several miles long and totally littered with dinosaur fossils. At Bone Cabin Quarry, Wyoming, the site was so abundant with dinosaur fossils that the excavators (1898) found that a sheepherder of earlier days had constructed a "log cabin" made entirely of dinosaur bones. The various digs at the Cleveland Lloyd Quarry in Utah, have yielded more than 12,000 bones which represent the remains of about 70 different animals, and 10 different kinds of dinosaurs. Dozens of complete skeletons and a large number of incomplete skeletons of the dinosaur *Coelophysis* have been excavated at the Ghost Ranch site in New Mexico. At Dinosaur National Monument, Utah, approximately 20 complete skeletons were extracted as well as bones and parts of skeletons representing nearly 300 individual dinosaurs. In the region of the Red Deer River in Alberta, Canada, the excavators, "...found fossil beds so rich that they could hardly move without stepping on the bones of herds of horned dinosaurs...." (David Lambert, *A Field Guide to Dinosaurs*, p. 22) At the site near Trossingen, Germany, thousands of plateosaur bones were discovered, representing at least 70 individuals. Many dinosaurs have also been found in various locations in Mongolia. In Tendaguru, Africa, the German expedition discovered another mass burial. In four years of excavating the workers were able to send back to Germany 250 tons of dinosaur bones.

These various mass burial sites indicate very strongly that the dinosaurs were the victims of a great flood which was global in extent and catastrophic in nature.

Today when animals die by predation or of natural deaths, it is not long before scavengers eat away the flesh and the bones oxidize and return to the soil. The presence of so many fossils of all kinds of creatures demonstrate that these bones were not exposed for a long period of time before burial. As Norman, for instance, states regarding the skeleton of a young camarosaur, a sauropod dinosaur, "The skeleton was preserved almost completely intact....It must be supposed that the carcass of this animal was buried very rapidly...." (David Norman, *The Illustrated Encyclopedia of Dinosaurs*, p. 86). In the past, and because of the global flood the animals must have been first drowned, and then quickly covered with sediments; otherwise, they would have soon decayed away, and we would have no opportunity to observe the kinds of animals which lived in the days of Noah.

Fossilized plants also tell us something of the kind of world that was here in the ancient past. If one takes time to explore the Gobi Desert of Mongolia, one will find it to be mostly a barren wasteland. Yet in different places great fossilized trees can be found there. These trees, plus the many plant eating dinosaurs which have been found there, suggest that in the past this was a land rich with vegetation. Further, some of the dinosaurs found there were of great size. By no means could they have survived in the Gobi if it had been in the past anything like it is today. Surely, the climate had to have been very much different than it is now, and very warm and conducive for the luxuriant growth of plants.

After the ark landed in the mountains of Ararat, the humans and the animals disembarked. Day by day thereafter, the animals began grazing their way across the expanse of the new world.   As they did they began to experience significant differences in the seasons for the first time. Weather and climate began to be much more noticeable than it had ever been before. Some animals, due to their particular biological make-up were able to go to almost every part of the new world. Cattle, horses, dogs, bear, and deer for instance are now found on the six major continents and in many different climactical situations. Others, such as wolves and beavers, found the temperate zones more to their liking.   Some were able to survive well in colder climates and still others, such as the elephant and the crocodile, were only able to do well in very warm climates.

Where then, one may ask, did the dinosaurs go if they did indeed survive the flood via the ark? This is a good question. We cannot answer it from a study of the fossils, for the fossils represent only the animals which died by means of Noah's flood. To answer this question we must survey the writings of ancient literature and the earliest accounts of human history after the Flood.   In this connection it is most interesting to note that the dinosaurs are mentioned in the Old Testament about 25 times as being in existence after the global Flood.   One of the most important references is found in the book of Job. In the 40th chapter we have a very fine description of a great sauropod dinosaur. The sauropods are generally divided into 6 separate families: the brachiosaurids, the camarasaurids, the cetiosaurids, the diplodocids, the titanosaurids, and the vulcanodontids. The sauropods are, of course, the great plant eating dinosaurs with the very long necks and tails.

It is just such an animal as these, which is mentioned in the 40th chapter of Job. "Behold now behemoth, which I made with thee; he eateth grass as an ox. He moveth his tail like a cedar..." (Job 40:15) There are a number of important concepts to be noted in this verse. 1) In Genesis 1:24 the word *behema* is translated "cattle." Actually, it probably refers to animals that are plant eaters. In the case of Job *behemoth* is the plural form of *behema*. Yet, as one can plainly see there is only one animal in context. However, in the Hebrew language the plural ending can also refer to intensity. Therefore, in Job 40:15 the language indicates that we have a very great animal indeed. 2) We see that God (here speaking in this verse to Job) makes it clear that He created behemoth along with Job. Now one may say that God did not make either Job or behemoth. God did make the early or original great reptiles and He did create Adam. So we see here, that God is the Creator, not merely of the first original generations of animal life, but of their descendants as well. That is, while, by means of sexual reproduction the species reproduce themselves through time. God is, nevertheless the source or Creator of the descendants. Behemoth was the descendant of the first dinosaurs. 3) We see that man and dinosaur were contemporaries in the days of Job, and thus, of necessity, in the world prior to the flood. 4) We find that this great animal was a plant eater. It has long been acknowledged that the sauropod dinosaurs were plant eaters. One look at their dentition makes that quite obvious. 5) We see that this animal had a tail like unto a cedar tree. Some commentators have tried to associate this word, with the elephant, but the elephant's tail will not quite fit the description here given. The only animal ever known to have a tail which fits this description is the sauropod dinosaur.

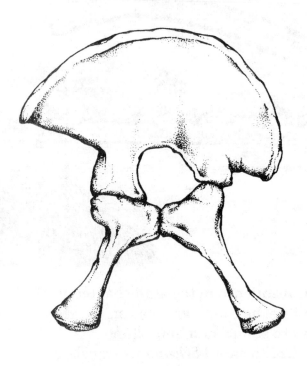

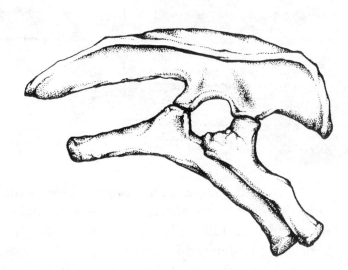

Saurischia   Ornithischia

Dinosaurs are actually divided into two separate orders: the saurischia and the ornithischia. The difference between the two has to do with the design of their hip. The saurischia have hips that are similar to those of lizards, while the ornithischia have hips which are somewhat similar to those of the bird. The saurischia are further divided into two subgroups: the sauropoda and the theropoda. The latter group, the theropoda, is the group which contains the dinosaurs which were carnivorous. These included such well known dinosaurs as *Tyrannosaurus*, *Allosaurus*, and *Megalosaurus*. The sauropods are sometimes referred to as the "gentle giants." They are known for their great size. They had bulky bodies with long necks and tails. They include such popular dinosaurs as *Brontosaurus* (now *Apatosaurus*), *Diplodocus*, and *Camarasaurus*. Their great size and extraordinarily long necks and tails easily distinguish them from the other dinosaurs.

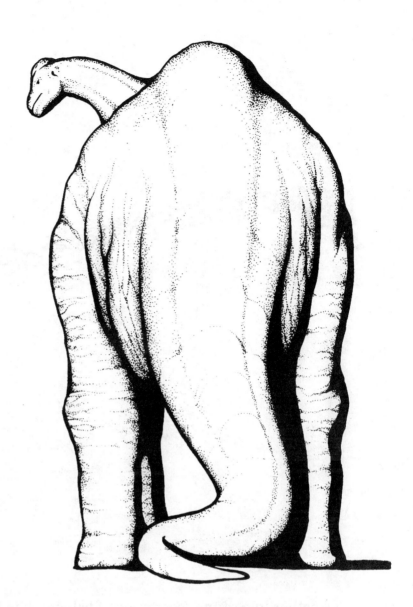
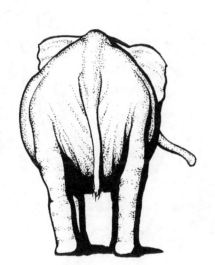

Speaking of the sauropod, *Apatosaurus,* here is a typical description, "The tail probably weighed several tons and may have balanced the animal when it walked. The length of the tail, around 30 feet to the tip, helped distribute the dinosaur's weight." (Peter Dodson [Consultant], *The Age of Dinosaurs,* pg. 52). A tail that is 30 feet long and that weighs several tons corresponds very favorably to the general description of a cedar tree. No other animal can fit this description. You may find that some of the older commentaries identify this animal as a large mammal, such as an elephant. However, the elephant as well as any of the large mammals have very short and thin tails which could not by any means correlate with the description in Job.

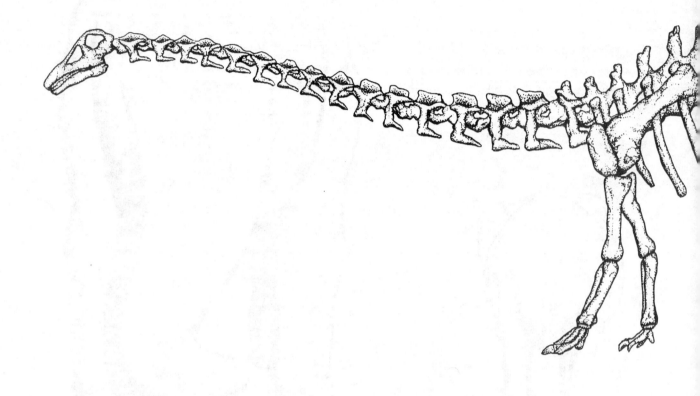

Another important description of behemoth is found in Job 40:18 where we read, "His bones are as strong pieces of brass; his bones are like bars of iron." Here we have two separate descriptions from two different phrases. In the Hebrew we find two different words for bones. The first is *etsem*, the common word for bones, and the second is *gerem,* a less common word for bones. This would seem to indicate that both the axial (vertebrae) and the appendicular (limbs) skeletons are being described. It is interesting to note that the ASV, NIV and others, translate the word *gerem* not as bones, but as limbs; referring, of course, to the various bones of the front and back legs. The previous descriptions of this animal in Job indicate a large and heavy animal. Thus, it would be necessary for the legs of such a giant to be very strong. The great sauropod dinosaurs such as *Apatosaurus* and *Brachiosaurus* weighed from 30 to 80 tons. This would necessitate leg bones being as "bars of iron."

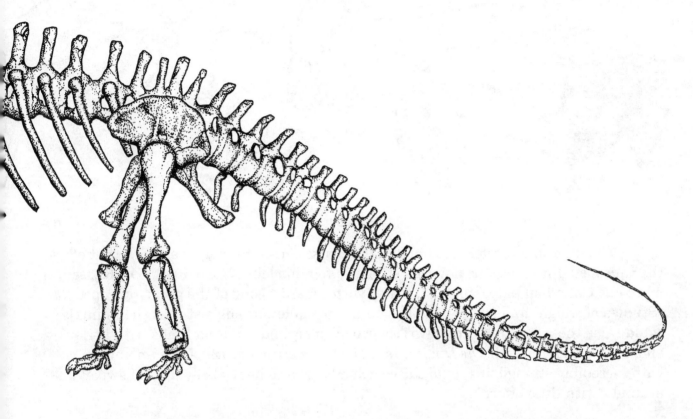

The KJV has translated the Hebrew words *aphiqey nechushah* as "pieces of brass," but the ASV, NIV and RSV have translated these words as "tubes of bronze." In Job's day, iron and bronze were the two strongest metals. These words may also be referring to the leg bones. If so, they would be emphasizing a second factor with regard to the structure of the leg bones, namely that in the case of the giant sauropod dinosaur's limb bones they were actually hollow rather than solid. On the other hand, these words may be referring to a second system of bones, the vertebral column. In this case, the word bronze would be most appropriate because bronze is more maleable than iron and speaks of flexibility, a factor that would be most important with regard to the maneuverability of the very long neck and tail of the sauropod dinosaur. The original meaning of the Hebrew word *aphiq* (tubes) actually means "channels" as when a ditch channels water from one place to another. In this case, the "tubes" or "channels" would refer to the strong, individual vertebrae through which the nerve cord stretched from the brain to the tail.

The description referenced in Job 40:16 also correlates very well with that of the sauropod dinosaur. "Lo now, his strength is in his loins." (Job 40:16) Dr. Russell, a famous Canadian paleontologist, states with regard to one of the great sauropods, "Studies of weight and stress distribution in the skeletons suggest that the animals could raise their forelimbs and pivot their bodies around the hind limbs with little effort." (Dale A. Russell, *The Dinosaurs of North America*, pg. 72.) Only an animal with incredibly strong loins could raise such a large and heavy body up and swivel it around "with little effort."

Further, it is interesting to note in this connection that the weight of today's large animals is evenly distributed upon all four legs. In the case of the sauropod dinosaur, however, it is acknowledged that the weight distribution is more toward the rear of the animal. This means, of course, that more weight would be borne up by "the loins." Jacobs, of Southern Methodist University, comments regarding the back legs of the sauropods, "They are generally quite a bit longer and more massive than the front legs, showing that the distribution of the weight in a sauropod body is shifted toward the back end. In bison or horses or camels...the front limb bones are more massive than the hind...." (Lewis Jacobs, *Quest for the African Dinosaur*, p. 128)

These various correlations of Job, chapter 40, with the fossil record should once and for all clarify that Bible commentators, who have suggested that the "behemoth" was an elephant or some other large mammal, are in error.

Now returning to our terms "tannin and tannim" we find that they are used about 25 times throughout the Old Testament from Genesis to Malachi. This indicates very clearly that these animals were very much alive during the time from Moses to the time of the prophet Malachi. The prophet Ezekiel speaks of "...the great dragon that lieth in the midst of his (Egypt's) rivers." (Ezekiel 29:3) A few years ago the San Francisco Chronicle announced, "American scientists have found dinosaur bones on a windswept mountain near the South Pole." In what kind of material were these dinosaur bones found? We are told they were found, "In large slabs of mudstone, formed from river sediments..." (San Francisco Chronicle, March 13, 1991). Many accounts of dinosaur discoveries are careful to note that such and such dinosaur was found in "river sediments". Again, for instance, we find reference to *Supersaurus* (a thirty ton sauropod) as a "...plant eating, river-wading giant...." (___ "Supersaurus", *Discover*, Sept. 1989). So then, it is quite in context that we should find Ezekiel referring to a "dragon" in the rivers of Egypt.

The prophet Micah refers to the sound system of two interesting animals as he attempts to communicate important truths to Israel. "I will make a wailing like the dragons, and mourning as the owls." (Micah 1:8) In support of this concept it is intriguing to learn that tannin (the Hebrew word for dragon/dinosaur) is constructed from a root word, *tnn*, which meant "to howl" (Brown, Drier, Briggs, *Hebrew and English Lexicon* s.v.). It is of further interest to consider in this connection the relatively recent discovery that the long hollow crest of the Lambeosaurine dinosaurs (*Lambeosaurus* and *Parasaurolophus*) were apparently used for the purpose of making sounds. "Lambeosaurine dinosaur crests are judged to have been conducive to resonation on the basis of an acoustic analysis of the structure of the nasal cavity." (David B. Weishampel, "Acoustic analysis of potential vocalization in lambeosaurine dinosaurs", *Paleobiology,* July 1981, pg. 252.) This research has been quickly integrated into the literature. Subsequently it is rather common to read accounts such as in the *Newsweek* article, "Listen closely and you can almost hear the ebbing surf...and the hooting, honking of dinosaurs that lived beside a sea...." (Sharon Begley and Emily Yoffee, "New Theories and Old Bones Reveal The Lifestyles of the Dinosaur," *Newsweek,* October 28, 1991).

It is also interesting to see that in the Old Testament "dragons" are often associated with judgment. Let us review three examples. First, speaking of the judgment against Jerusalem, we read, "For the mountains will I take up a weeping and wailing, and for the habitations of the wilderness a lamentation, because they are burned up, so that none can pass through them; neither can men hear the voice of the cattle; both the fowl of the heavens and the beast are fled; they are gone, and I will make Jerusalem heaps, and a den of dragons; and I will make the cities of Judah desolate, without an inhabitant" (Jeremiah 9:10, 11). Apart from highlighting the fact that dragons are at times associated with judgment, these verses also underscore the fact that dragons are mentioned along with other basic animal kinds and are shown to be distinct from cattle, birds, and the ordinary beasts of the field.

Second, we have dragons associated with the judgement of Babylon. After the death of Solomon, Israel was split into two kingdoms: the Northern Kingdom under the rule of Jeroboam, and the Southern Kingdom under the rule of Rehoboam. The Northern Kingdom (historically known as Israel), whose capital was in Samaria, lasted until 722 B.C. when, because of their idolatry and unrighteous behavior, they were taken into captivity by Assyrians. This is recorded in the book of II Kings, "And they left all the commandments of the Lord their God, and made them molten images, even two calves, and made a grove, and worshipped all the host of heaven and served Baal." (II Kings 17:16) The Southern Kingdom (historically known as Judah), continued on for many years, due in part to a number of good kings who worshiped the Lord and revered His word. Among these were Joash, Josiah, and Hezekiah. However, many of the kings, in the Davidic line, led Israel astray and caused the citizens of this country to worship false gods. Though many prophets of God, such as Isaiah and Jeremiah, were used to warn Israel of the coming dangers, their advice was largely unheeded. As a result God allowed the kingdom of Judah to be taken in captivity by the Babylonians.

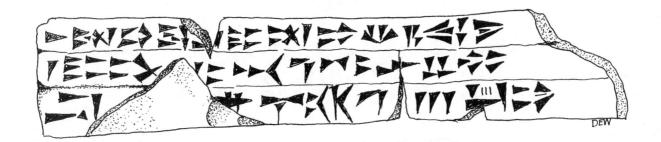

In the year 597 B.C. Nebuchadnezzar captured the city of Jerusalem. At this time, many Jewish captives were taken away to Babylon, including Daniel, who wrote in his book, "In the third year of the reign of Jehoiakim king of Judah came Nebuchadnezzar king of Babylon unto Jerusalem, and besieged it. And the Lord gave Jehoiakim king of Judah into his hand..." (Dan. 1:1-2) As the result of a later rebellion by the Jews led by Zedekiah, Nebuchadnezzar came again and destroyed the city and temple of Jerusalem. After Nebuchadnezzar conquered Jerusalem and Israel, he began to make improvements in the city of Babylon and to strengthen its defenses. Archaeologists, in the 19th century were able to find and excavate much of the ruins of Babylon. On the Ishtar Gate, they found the following words written. Translated into English they say,

"Babylon, the exalted city, the city of the god Marduk....
At the entrance of its gates, I set massive bulls and fiersome dragons...."
        (Nebuchadnezzar II 604-562 B.C.)

Nebuchadnezzar himself actually became a true worshipper of the Lord God of Israel. However, those who came after him turned away from the Lord God unto pagan deities. In fact, in the days of Belshazzer, they also showed great contempt for the name of the Lord at a banquet by drinking wine from the sacred vessels taken from the temple in Jerusalem. Long before this time, God, knowing the tendency of the Babylonian kings and people, spoke a prophecy through Jeremiah regarding the judgement, which would fall upon Babylon, "And Babylon shall become heaps, a dwelling place for dragons, an astonishment, and an hissing without an inhabitant." (Jer. 51:37). Now, in modern times, having read the Biblical text regarding these things, and having excavated the city of Babylon, we find that the once proud walls did indeed contain pictures of wild bulls and fierce dragons. Also, as we view the broken walls and rubble, we find that Babylon did indeed, according to the word of the Lord, become a "place of heaps." Undoubtedly for many years thereafter, it was also a habitation of dragons.

Third, in Malachi 1:3 we read, "And I hated Esau, and laid his mountains and his heritage waste for the dragons of the wilderness." With regard to the concept of judgment it is interesting to note that most of the dinosaurs were actually plant eaters. The fossil record also shows that dinosaurs had the tendency to herd together. Some of these herds were amazingly large. In the finds made at Egg Mountain, Montana, Dr. John Horner reports, "At a conservative estimate, we had found the tomb of a herd of ten thousand dinosaurs." (John Horner, *Digging Dinosaurs*, pg. 128). It would not do to turn over a region in judgment to the wolves of the wilderness, for they eat meat and would do little damage to the flora. To lay it waste for the dragons however, seeing that most of them were plant eaters would make much more sense. Second, this passage is also important from the standpoint of time. Malachi is the last book of the Old Testament. It was written about 400 years before the advent of Christ. This indicates very clearly then that reptilian like beings then referred to as "dragons" were alive and flourishing about 400 BC. This is in sharp conflict with the Evolutionary Geologic Column which places dinosaurs on the earth from about 220 million to 65 million years ago.

It is of interest also to note that at approximately the same time that the book of Malachi was being written, the dragon had already become an important artistic motif in the land of China. The sauropod dinosaurs such as *Apatosaurus* and *Brachiosaurus*, had five toes on their feet. Other dinosaurs had less. It is significant to note that in China the motif of the five-toed dragon had become the symbol of the imperial government. "The five-clawed feet of the dragon identify him as a symbol of the emperor, the Son of Heaven. Nonimperial dragons had four claws." (C.J. Fitzgerald, *The Horizon History of China*, 1969, pg. 73)

The accounts just quoted are from the Sacred Scripture. These accounts represent a high degree of credibility because it was important to the Creator, and the God of Israel to communicate His truth and to see that it was accurately preserved for all generations. In addition to these accounts, however we have other accounts from the secular world. We are not authorized to believe that God has insured their accuracy. Nevertheless, there are so very many of them, it seems most reasonable to believe that these ancient people were writing about animals which really existed. According to their descriptions the only animals it would seem that they could be referring to are the ones which we find in the fossil record today and which are now identified as dinosaurs.

In AD 70, at the time of the fall of Jerusalem, Pliny finished his famous Natural History. In it he stated, "Africa produces elephants, but it is India that produces the largest, as well as the dragon..." (Pliny, *Natural History*, 70 AD) Pliny is one of the ancient world's most famous and most reliable writers. It seems apparent that in his era, dragons were known to be alive in India. It is also of importance to note here, that when bringing in the concept of the dragon, Pliny seems to associate the size factor of the dragon with our largest animal extant today--the elephant.

Aelian, in his *De Natura Animalium*, written about A.D. 220, says, "The Phrygian History also states that dragons are born which reach ten paces in length...." Ten paces is about 25 to 30 feet. This would indeed have been a large animal--a large reptilian-like animal. In size it would correspond favorably with many of the medium to large sized dinosaurs. These would include *Triceratops*, *Ankylosaurus*, and *Plateosaurus*.

Jordanus in his book, *The Wonders of the East* (550 A.D.) reports, "These dragons grow exceeding big, and from their mouths cast forth a most pestilential breath..." The idea that large reptilian-like animals may have had odorous breath does not seem unreasonable, either. Yet, more important than this, is the time factor here. In the year of this book's publication, 550 A.D., the world had already seen the passing of the Roman empire. It was now starting into the Dark Ages. Jordanus gives two characteristics of these animals: they had pestilential breath, and they were very large. The fossil evidence cannot tell us much about their breath, but it certainly indicates that they were large.

Now with regard to the association of the words "tannim" with "dragons," I agree with the comments of Dr. Henry Morris. Dr. Morris is a highly regarded scholar, a prolific writer and the past president of the Institute of Creation Research, he states, "...if one will simply translate *tannim* by 'dinosaurs' every one of the more than twenty-five uses of the word becomes perfectly clear and appropriate." (Henry M. Morris, *The Biblical Basis for Modern Science* p. 352)

Then with regard to the association of "dragons" with "dinosaurs" I also agree with the comments of Dr. Dong Zhiming. Dr. Zhiming is China's leading paleontologist and the author of the book, *Dinosaurs From China*. He states, "The interpretation of dinosaurs as dragons goes back more than two thousand years in Chinese culture...." (Dong Zhiming, *Dinosaurs from China* p. 9) Another popular book adds to this. This book, *The Age of the Dinosaurs* has for its consultant, Dr. Peter Dodson of the University of Pennsylvania, one of the more popular writers and scholars on the subject of dinosaurs. This book states, "Dinosaurs have been associated with dragons for a long time. *Mamenchisaurus* was discovered at a collection site for 'dragon bones'...." (*Age of Dinosaurs* p. 73) *Mamenchisaurus* has become a record holder. This long and slender, 20 ton sauropod was approximately 70 feet long. It was an amazing thing for the paleontologists who excavated this great dinosaur to find that the neck was actually half of the total body length.

It seems apparent that the Chinese for the last 2000 years have had no difficulty identifying the bones of the great animals which they believe to be of medicinal value. *The Age of Dinosaurs* further states, "The Chinese thought their dinosaur's bones were dragon remains and ground them up for sale in drug stores." (*The Age of Dinosaurs* consultant: Peter Dodson, Ph. D., Publications International, Ltd., 1993, p. 73) To them, these were the bones of dragons. Today, those same bones are identified by leading paleontologists as dinosaur bones. It is not, therefore, an unreasonable suggestion to make that dinosaurs and dragons are essentially the same animals.

The dinosaur fossils represent the remains of the dinosaurs which died by means of the great world wide Flood, referenced in the book of Genesis. The dragon stories, however, represent accounts of dinosaurs which were seen by the descendants of Noah's family for many years after the great Flood.

After hundreds of years, the great reptilian-like creatures were seen by fewer and fewer people. Eventually, dragons became the subjects of storytelling by the aging parents and grandparents. For a variety of reasons the great dragons began to die out. In some cases it was because of the weather and climate. In others because of the change in the amount of oxygen in the air. In still many others it was because the people, migrating across the new earth, developed an increasingly hostile attitude toward lizards of great size. They were doubtless seen as threats to the families and to the crops of these new migrants. After so long a time they were hunted to extinction. The civilized peoples wanted lands filled with crops and cattle, not with plant eating, much less, meat eating lizards equal in size to their cattle and goats.

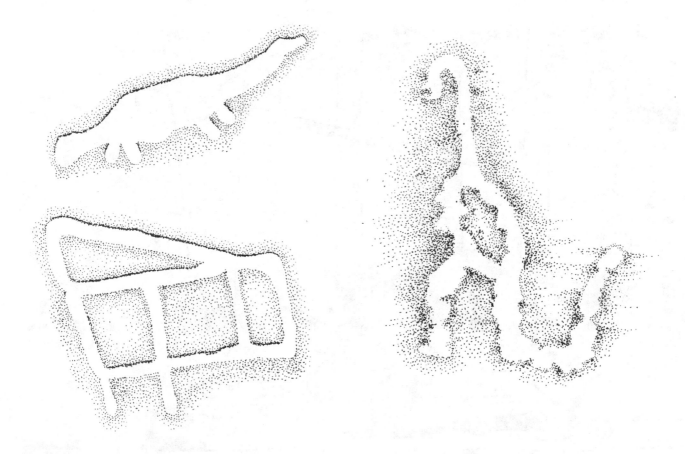

Nevertheless, in certain areas of the earth, especially those that were warmer year round, some of the great dragons were able to perpetuate their kind a little farther down the road of history. Now and then, the humans which either lived in these areas or occasionally traveled through them, would see the rare sight of the giant reptile. A few of these observers have left a record of the animals which they saw. One, in particular, is to be found in Arizona. In this case one of the ancient Indians which inhabited this land hundreds of years ago recorded his observation on a cliff wall. The animal he saw looks exactly like a species of dinosaur which modern artists have drawn after observing the fossil bones. In 1925, an expedition from the Oakland Museum of California came to observe these various petroglyphs. Included among the pictures that they took, is one that looks very much like a dinosaur. The animal is standing upright on its hind legs and using its long tail as a sort of tripod. Shortly after their return the accomplishments and observations of this expedition were written up in a museum publication. The following is their comment made in this report in regard to this animal which looks very much like a dinosaur. "The fact that the animal is upright and balanced on its tail would seem to indicate that the prehistoric artist must have seen it alive." (*Discoveries Relating To Prehistoric Man*, Oct. 1924, Oakland Museum, Director of Expedition: Samuel Hubbard.)

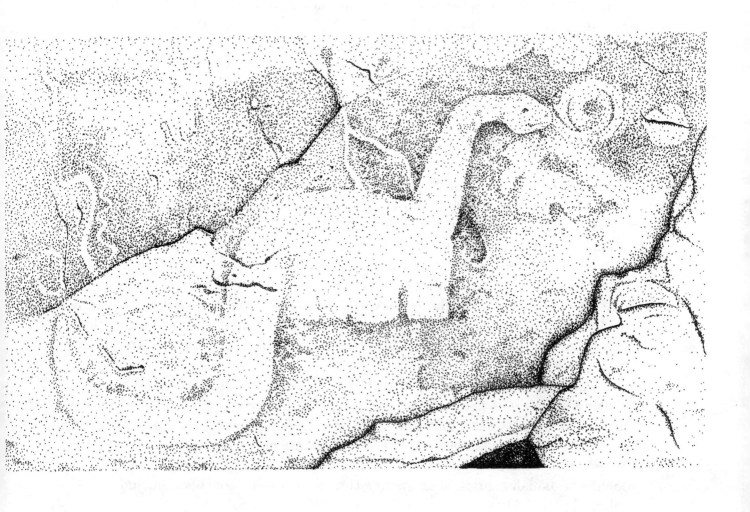

Other petroglyphs also reflect that ancient people in North America were quite familiar with the animal which today we identify as the dinosaur. Underneath one of the amazing rock bridges in White Rock Canyon, Utah there is another such petroglyph. This time the dinosaur is very clearly a sauropod like *Apatosaurus* (*Brontosaurus*) or *Camarasaurus*. This particular petroglyph has been attributed to the work of the ancient Anasazi Indians who lived in this area from approximately 400 A.D. to 1300 A.D. From the book *Prehistoric Indians* we read, "There is a petroglyph in Natural Bridges National Monument that bears a startling resemblance to a dinosaur, specifically a Brontosaurus, with a long tail and neck, small head and all." (*Prehistoric Indians*, Barnes and Pendleton, 1995, p. 201)

In 1945, in Mexico, a German hardware merchant named Mr. Waldermar Julsrud, discovered a small figurine near a dry ditch. Upon careful investigation he realized that it was unlike any of the artifacts that had previously been discovered. Julsrud was very familiar with Aztec, Toltec, Inca and other ancient Indian artifacts. This, he realized was different from all of the rest. He soon assigned one of his workers the task of unearthing as many of these figurines as he could find. At the end of approximately 3 years the cache of figurines, ranging from several inches to 6 feet in size, reached the amazing quantity of approximately 32,000 objects.

Julsrud endeavored to interest archaeologists to come and review his collection as it began developing. Eventually the collection came to the attention of Charles H. Hapgood, author of the rather famous book, *Maps of Ancient Sea Kings.* In due time, to verify the authenticity of this discovery, Hapgood in turn obtained the investigative ability of the famous lawyer and novelist, Earl Stanley Gardner. Mr. Gardner was a defense attorney who became Public Prosecutor of Los Angeles County. He is probably better known for his successful Perry Mason detective series. Hapgood states, "From the photo sent him Mr. Gardner said it was obvious that no one individual or group could have made these pieces." (*Mystery in Acambaro*, p. 9).

Tinajero, the worker hired to dig up the objects, found that they had been apparently purposely buried in pits containing 20-40 objects per pit. The figurines were made of ceramic, jade, stone and obsidian. They represented a variety of ethnic groups. Eventually it was reasoned that this very ancient tribe had hastily buried the cherished representations of their culture in order to protect them from the approaching Spanish armies. This means that they would have been buried somewhere in the 1600's.

This amazing collection consisted of a large variety of animals which lived in both the present and the past. Some of the reptiles looked very much like the ancient dinosaurs. This lead Julsrud to the conclusion that in the past humans and dinosaurs had been contemporaries. As a result of such articles being published in the Mexican press, the archeological establishment, oriented to the theory of evolution, refused to take the discovery seriously.

Hapgood took many pictures of these figurines and included some of them in his book *Mystery in Acambaro*. In picture #30, we have "...a representation of the extinct American camel-llama." Picture #29 shows a "...bird, a giant monkey, a llama, two probably imaginary animals, two giant monkeys, and an accurate representation of the North American dinosaur, Brachiosaurus."

After sighting cases of animals that theoretically lived millions of years ago and are living today such as the coelacanth and the horseshoe crab, he argues that, "Because dinosaurs died out in other parts of the world a long time ago there is no rule of nature that says that they may not have survived in Mexico until quite recently. We shall examine photographs of several figurines that strongly suggest that they did."

Hapgood's scientific orientation is clearly in support of the theory of evolution as evidenced by such remarks as "We know, for example, that birds developed from reptiles in the Mesozoic Era and that many dinosaurs had birdlike characteristics." (Mystery in Acambaro, page 6). Nevertheless he also reports, "...Ivan T. Sanderson, the naturalist, found one accurate representation of a known dinosaur in the collection. Oddly enough, this was the American dinosaur, the Brachiosaurus, not at all well-known to the public. Sanderson wrote me about this figurine and said in part, 'this figurine is in that very fine, jet-black, polished-looking ware. It is about a foot tall. The point is, it is an absolutely perfect representation of Brachiosaurus, known only from East Africa and North America. There are a number of outlines of the skeletons in the standard literature but only one fleshed-out reconstruction that I have ever seen. This statuette is exactly like it.' " (Ibid.)

Hapgood reports that this collection represents a very primitive Indian culture and the dating methods used imply that this culture goes back at least before the time of Christ. He also states, "The presence of extinct animals and the evidence of the radiocarbon and thermoluminescent dates suggests that this was the seminal culture whose influence spread throughout all Indian America." (page 11)

This evidence then, strongly suggests that this is a genuine collection of artifacts representing a very ancient Indian culture. How could these ancient Indians know of the now extinct camel-llama and of the dinosaur unless they had seen them or had been told of them by their elders. This collection provides more significant evidence that the evolutionary time scale, with regard to the extinction of dinosaurs and other ancient animals, is in error.

In time only the fossils of the animals which perished in the great Flood mentioned in the book of Genesis remained to remind people of the size and kinds of animals of the First World. For many years even these fossilized bones were generally unnoticed. Here and there, groups of people, as in the aforementioned account of the Chinese, might find some use for them, but for the most part they were either unnoticed or ignored. Part of the reason for this is that very often these dinosaur fossils were found in remote regions where city dwellers and members of the farming community were not likely to visit. On the other hand these sedimentary deposits containing the dinosaur fossils had become, by the time of the modern era, overlaid with soil. Consequently, farmers in many cases have been plowing the soil for years which may have been from three to ten feet or more above the fossiliferous sedimentary rocks. Thus, for so very many years, only men crossing the wilderness as trappers or hunters might have stumbled across a dinosaur fossil. They would have no idea what animal it represented. If they guessed at all, they would have envisaged a large edition of one of today's animals.

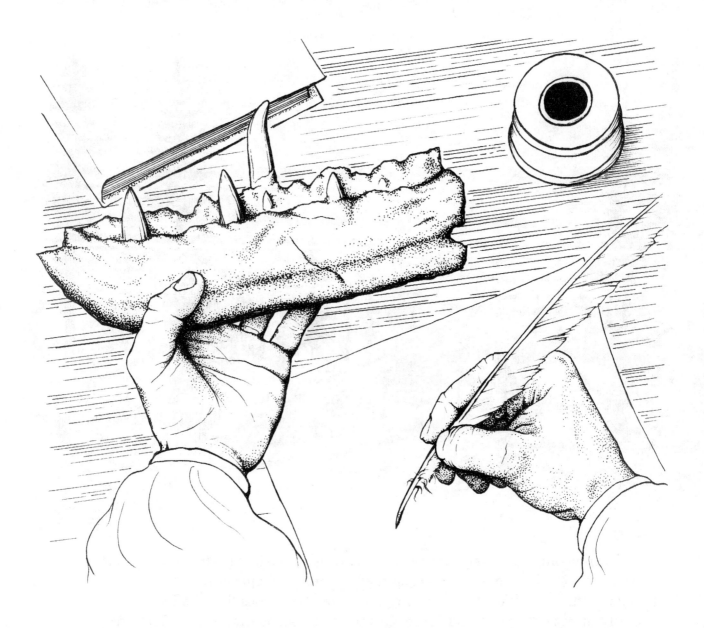

Finally, in the 1700's and 1800's it became of interest to certain educated citizens of England and Western Europe to collect fossils. These proved to be fascinating items for collection. Through the discovery and study of these fossils, scholarly men attempted to understand the nature of Creation and to answer various important questions about origins and the early life of this planet. Among those who adopted this hobby was William Buckland, who was an Anglican priest and professor of Geology at Oxford. Eventually, Buckland was presented with a most unique fossil. This was a large lower jaw of an animal which according to Buckland appeared to be quite reptilian. In his 1824 description of it, he referred to it as the "great reptile from Stonesfield" because it had been found near the English town of Stonesfield.

A medical doctor named Gideon Mantell had also taken up the hobby of
collecting fossils. The story is told that one day he and his wife Mary were making a
call on a patient who lived in the country. While Gideon was visiting with the
patient, Mary got out of the buggy and began searching around a pile of gravel. Soon
she discovered some fossil fragments. Among them was a part of a very large tooth.
When she showed it to Gideon, he was elated. He took it back to town and began
showing it around to his different intellectual friends. Dr. Mantell was certain that
it was unique, a very important find. He was sure that it was from a reptile.
Unfortunately, when he shared it with his friends, none but Dr. Walliston could be
found to agree with him. Some dismissed it as being of little consequence, and
most refused to believe that it was reptilian.

Finally, Dr. Mantell took the tooth to the great Museum of Natural History in London. He went up and down the rows of drawers trying to find a jaw to which this unusual tooth would fit. He was unsuccessful in his quest. However, after a while he began chatting with a student who had been studying in Central America. When Dr. Mantell showed this student the tooth, the student, Stutchbury, stated that it was quite like the teeth of the iguana lizards he had seen in Central America. This was what Mantell needed to hear. Now he was even more confident that these teeth were from a giant, yet now extinct reptile.

Later more of the skeleton was found and scientists were then able to reconstruct this strange, ancient creature. As suggested it turned out to be a most unique and truly giant reptile. Dr. Mantell gave it the name *Iguanodon* which means "iguana tooth." Since then many fossils of this animal have been found and it has become one of the more popularly known dinosaurs.

By and by the interest in fossils increased. And, consequently, more and more were found. Included among the new discoveries were the fossils of more animals which again appeared to be reptilian in nature. In 1832, fossils of yet another large lizard-like animal were discovered in the Tilligate Forest area in Sussex, England. This creature was quite unique in that it was evident from the fossils that this was actually an armored animal. In life it would have been seen as a 13 to 16 foot long thorny giant waddling about without fear of carnivores. Its back was covered by a tough hide. Rows of sharp spikes stuck out from the neck, shoulders and back. Smaller circular plates covered the tail. It was described by Dr. Gideon Mantell, and received the name *Hylaeosaurus* or "woodland lizard."

In 1836 another one of these unusual animals was found. It was about 7 feet in length and it had a long neck and tail and was named with reference to its unusual teeth. It received the name *Thecodontosaurus* or "socket-toothed lizard." The fossils of this small reptile, found in the Keuper Beds in England, indicated that this creature was bipedal, that is, it walked mainly on its hindlimbs. Its slender forearms were shorter than the hindlimbs and its hands were long and narrow.

In 1841, new bones were found. They were so large that at first they were thought to be those of a whale. Eventually, they were seen to be those of a reptile which was given the name *Cetiosaurus* or "whale lizard."

With so many of these unusual beasts now found in fossil form it seemed necessary to place them in one or another scientific category. The whole collection was turned over to England's leading anatomist, Dr. Richard Owen. He was convinced, as were many of the real scientists of his day, that the sedimentary layers containing fossils were here by means of Noah's flood. After comparing the fossil reptiles with the bones of reptilian animals which had died in the zoo, Dr. Owen was able to discern that they were all to be placed in the class Reptilia. His harder problem was the placing of them in their proper Order. The class reptilia had at that time four separate orders: one containing the serpents, one containing the alligators, one containing the turtles and one containing the lizards. The order containing the lizards was called Sauria.

It was obvious to Dr. Owen that these newly found fossils were quite similar to the lizards in their anatomy. Yet, it did not seem fitting to place them in that order, since they were of such great size and since there were some very significant anatomical differences. Thus, in 1842 he created a new order for them and gave them their new scientific name: dinosauria or "terrible lizards." Because it was found that there were significant differences in the many fossils found, they were actually assigned to two separate orders now known as the Saurischia (lizard-hipped) and the Ornithischia (bird-hipped) dinosaurs.

We see then that these animals are traceable right back to the beginning of time both by means of the fossil record, which essentially contains the bones of animals killed and buried during the time of Noah's flood, and by means of God's revelation. We find that they were the products of God's creation just as were all of the other animals. We find further that, regardless of the evolutionary claim that dinosaurs became extinct 65 million years ago, they were seen by reliable eye witnesses at least as recently as the time of Malachi, 400 years before the birth of Christ.

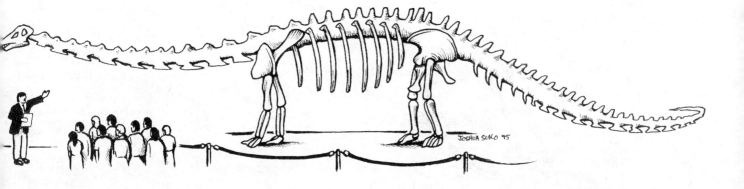

From the Scriptures, from historic accounts of the various cultures of the
world, and from the fossil evidence, we find that these most unusual animals are not
the evolutionary descendants of lower reptiles. Further they did not become extinct
because of a meteorite or comet hitting the earth. Nor did they live on the earth
millions of years ago. Instead we find that the dinosaurs found today in fossil form,
were essentially the same creatures historically referred to as dragons. The dragons
were simply the dinosaurs which, by means of Noah's ark, survived the Flood.   The
fossils of the dinosaurs which we now study are, in fact, the "tannim" referred to
about 25 times throughout the Old Testament. The hint of the eventual demise of
the great dragons was recorded in the book of Job when God was showing behemoth
to Job for an audio visual lesson of God's great power. "...He that made him can
make his sword to approach unto him." (Job 40:19). This appears to be the only
time in God's revelation in which the threat of extinction is directed toward a
member of the animal species. This then, along with the various and sundry facts
connected to these great creatures, tends to make them one of the most mysterious
animals of all time—the tannim, the dragons, the dinosaurs.

Sea Dragons

Mary Anning, of Lyme Regis, England, was one of the first successful collectors of fossil ichthyosaurs (swimming reptiles) and pterosaurs (flying reptiles). Fourteen years before Professor Buckland named the first dinosaur (*Megalosaurus*), this young girl who lived near the Dorset coast of England discovered her first sea dragon—a swimming reptile, known to us as an ichthyosaur.

The ichthyosaur was a unique reptile, which was designed by the Creator to live in the sea. Being reptiles and not fish, they had to frequently come up for air. Nevertheless, they were expert swimmers endowed with a marvelous capacity to obtain prey such as ammonites. Among the features given them to insure success in their world were a vertical tail fin, which was effective in developing speed, a fin on top of the body used to keep the reptile upright, fin paddles for steering and propulsion, and a long tapered head with very sharp teeth. Generally speaking, they were similar in shape to our modern day dolphin. These reptiles did not lay eggs, instead their young were born alive in the sea. In length these amazing reptiles range from 10 to 50 feet. Many ichthyosaurs have been found. In fact, about 3,000 have been found in Germany alone.

Since the days of Mary Anning of Lyme Regis, England, many ichthyosaur specimens have been found in widely separated areas of the world. *Mixosaurus* was first found in Switzerland and in northern Italy. This species, relatively small in size, was fishlike in appearance and possessed large eye orbits.

The 16 foot long *Ophthalmosaurus* or "eye lizard" is the species with the largest eyes. It has been suggested that this anatomical feature enabled *Ophthalmosaurus* to hunt its prey in deeper water or in the evening.

Cymbospondylus or "boat vertebrate" was a robustly built, 32 foot long ichthyosaur with a skull measuring 36 inches. The long, narrow jaws contained many sharp, conical teeth.

Shonisaurus (above), which was named for the Shoshone Mountains, is an important species of ichthyosaur to the fossil record for two reasons. First, at 50 feet in length, and weighing an estimated 20 to 35 tons, it is to date the largest of the ichthyosaurs. The forelimbs and hindlimbs were approximately six feet in length. Second, the discovery of more than 30 fossilized skeletons near Berlin, Nevada represent yet another fine example of mass burials. About 37 individuals of *Shoinsaurus popularis* have been unearthed.

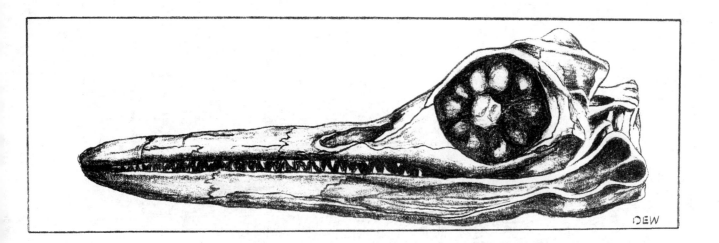

The first scientist to describe ichthyosaurs was Dr. William Buckland, professor of Geology at Oxford. Dr. Buckland had respect for God as Creator and spoke of the various unique aspects of the ichthyosaurs within the framework of intelligent design. We find that the ichthyosaur had large ear bones, indicating that they had a good sense of hearing. These ear bones were able to carry sound vibrations from both air and water to the inner ear. The eye sockets were very large, indicating that they may have hunted at dusk or in deeper water. In one specimen, the eye orbit was four inches in diameter. The eyeballs were surrounded by a ring of bones, the sclerotic ossicle, which probably protected their eyes when diving abruptly for prey. Buckland states, "...the preservation of this curiously constructed hoop of bony plates, shews that the enormous eye, of which they formed the front, was an optical instrument of varied and prodigious power, enabling the Ichthyosaurus to descry its prey at great or little distances, in the obscurity of night, and in the depths of the sea..." (William Buckland, *Geology and Mineralogy, Considered with Reference to Natural Theology*, volume 1, William Pickering, 1836, p. 174.)

It has also been suggested that this ring of bones was useful for protecting the eye from being slapped by the small waves whenever this dragon of the sea surfaced. They may have also given the eyes of the ichthyosaurs both microscopic and telescopic powers. "In living animals these bony plates are fixed in the exterior or sclerotic coat of the eye, and vary its scope of action, by altering the convexity of the cornea: by their retraction they press forward the front of the eye and convert it into a telescope." (Ibid., p. 174.)

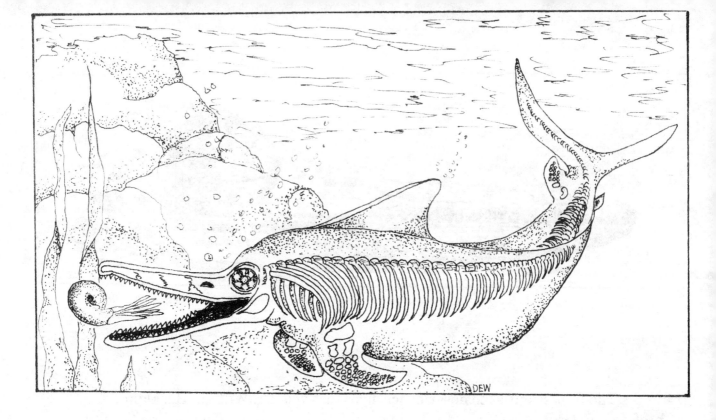

The snout was elongated which gave it a porpoise-like appearance. The long jaws were not composed of one long bone. If they had been, the lower jaw could have been fractured when the jaws had to snap shut on a squirming prey. Instead they were composed of several smaller bones. Dr. Buckland comments, "This contrivance in the lower jaw, to combine the greatest elasticity and strength with the smallest weight of materials, is similar to that adopted in binding together several parallel plates of elastic wood...to make a crossbow.... As in the...compound bow, so also in the compound jaw of the Ichthyosaurus, the plates are most numerous and strong, at the parts where the greatest strength is required to be exerted; and are thinner, and fewer, towards the extremities, where the service to be performed is less severe." (Ibid., p.176.)

One of the reasons that sea dragons were seen less frequently is because they were able to stay underwater for long periods of time made possible by the design of their ribs. The ribs of the right side were united to those of the left by a set of intermediate bones which came to be referenced as the *"sterno-costal"* arcs. "This structure was probably subservient to the purpose of introducing to their bodies an unusual quantity of air; the animal by this means being enabled to remain long beneath the water, without rising to the surface for the purpose of breathing." (Ibid., p. 180.) Ichthyosaurs had both paddles (flippers) and fins. The fins probably were used for stabilization and steering and the paddles for lift, but neither were used for propulsion. This was accomplished by the tail, swishing back and forth rapidly which may have allowed it to swim at speeds up to 40 miles per hour.

In 1830, Charles Lyell, a lawyer, wrote his now famous *Principles of Geology*. Lyell, who saw no conflict between creation and evolution, was of the opinion that the earth was exceedingly old. He was adamantly opposed to the Mosaic record, especially inasmuch as this record indicated that the earth was relatively young. However, it was generally accepted among scientists at that time that the Noahic flood was primarily responsible for the vast deposits of sedimentary rocks in which these new fossils were being found. Lyell was opposed to this idea. In his presentation of uniformitarianism he argued that these sedimentary layers had developed slowly and gradually in a uniform manner over millions of years of time. The effect of his work was to undermine the integrity of the book of Genesis and to pave the way for the people of England and Europe to more readily accept Darwin's views of evolution. In a sense, we might say that Lyell's *Principles of Geology* was the foundation upon which Darwin's *Origin of Species* was successfully constructed.

As a result of Lyell's ideas of uniformitarianism and Charles Suchirt's work, scientists, accepting the idea of evolution and long ages for the history of the earth, believe that each foot of sedimentary rock represents from about 1,500 to 3,000 years of time. If these ideas are accepted then we are obligated to believe that an animal whose bones were a few inches in diameter, must have taken about 1,000 years to be covered by sediments and to fossilize. This, however, is quite contrary to the facts, since it is obvious that the body of an animal would decay in a short period of time and there would be no carcass to fossilize. In order for any of the animals in the fossil record to be fossilized they had to be quickly covered by sediments. Otherwise, the carcasses would decay, oxidize and return to the soil.

It is of interest to note that in order for Lyell to make the case for uniformitarianism in his book, *Principles of Geology*, he had to disregard the innumerable evidences of catastrophism which are found in the sedimentary rocks and fossil records.

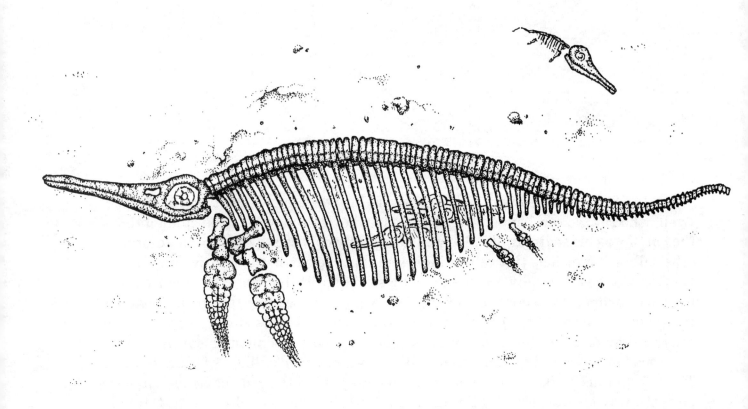

Many ichthyosaurs have been discovered in fossil form since Mary Anning's first find. Among these, at least 50 have been found to have young ichthyosaurs in their rib cages. This has given rise to a serious debate among paleontologists. Some have insisted that the young were the prey of the ichthyosaur. This meant, of course, that the ichthyosaurs were to be regarded as cannibals. Other paleontologists have argued that the young were actually the unborn infants. The research of Roland Bottcher in recent times has gone far to establish the idea that these young were indeed embryos. Among the clues leading to this conclusion is the observation that the heads of the young are almost always pointing forward. Most modern animals which swallow their prey whole generally swallow them head first. It is unlikely in such cases that the swallowed prey would all wind up pointing forward in the gut of the predator. Further, the young of these fossil ichthyosaurs appear to be located more nearly in the uterus than in the gut. The young of our modern whales and hippos are born tail first. For animals confined to water, the tail first birth has an obvious advantage. It allows the embryo to receive from the mother's supply of oxygen right up to the last second before birth.

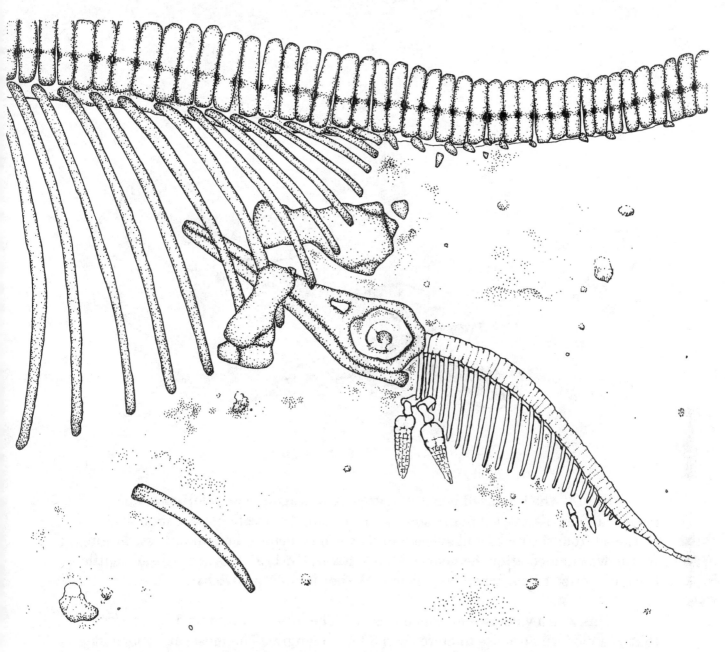

Since the time of Lyell, a very large amount of evidence has accumulated which undermines the theory of uniformitarianism and the idea that the earth is millions of years old. One of the many evidences for catastrophism is to be found in the case of an ichthyosaur fossilized while in the process of giving birth. Benton reports, "In some cases the embryo's head remains lodged between the pelvic bones, while its body lies outside." (Michael Benton, "The Myth of Mesozoic Cannibals" *New Scientist*, October 12, 1991, pg. 40) In these cases the young were in the process of being born. However, before they could swim away they, along with their mother, were incarcerated in the sediments. This undoubtedly speaks of rapid rather than slow and gradual sedimentation.

In 1780 the fossilized bones of a great sea dragon, now referred to as a mosasaur was discovered in present day Holland. An excellent specimen was retrieved from the rocks and subsequently reconstructed. This unique swimming reptile was named after the nearby Meuse River. In 1795 this great fossil reptile became a prize of war when Napoleon took the city of Maastricht.

This was a vicious sea dragon indeed. The mosasaurs ranged in size from that of a modern porpoise to more than 30 ft. in length. The mosasaur was a long snake-like sea reptile, which had a large skull and a long large jaw containing many slightly recurved teeth. The jaw was unusual in that it not only hinged in the back as in the case of modern reptiles, but there was also a joint halfway back from the end of the snout in the lower jaw. This extra joint, which was connected with ligaments, allowed the jaw to open even wider. The mosasaur probably fed on ammonites and a variety of fish.

For locomotion it had four paddle-like appendages. The toes and fingers were long and slender and probably webbed. Its long broad tail was also useful in achieving rapid propulsion through the water. The long flexible backbone contained 100 vertebrae.

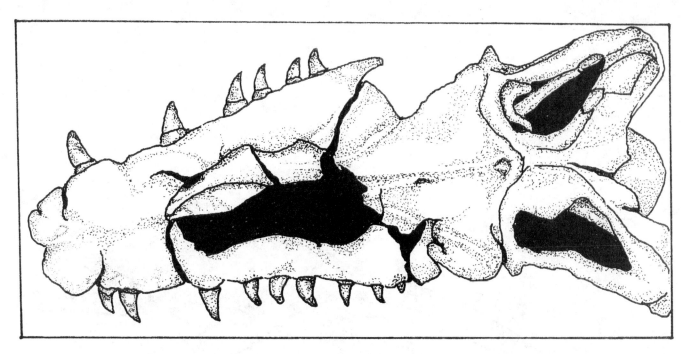

Platecarpus

Halisaurus or "sea lizard" was a species of mosasaur, about 10 to 13 feet in length, which had a thick, eel-like body with a long, flat tail. Its large, powerful jaws possess many short teeth. The teeth design of mosasaurs made it possible for them to seize and crush their prey. The jaws have flexible joints, which allowed them to open wide. It seems apparent that mosasaur also fed on ammonites. In Alberta, Canada thousands of ammonite shells have been found in association with many mosasaur fossil.

Tylosaurus or "swollen lizard" was a giant mosasaur about 30 feet in length with a four foot long jaw. The "Bunker Mosasaur" was a tylosaur whose skull was about six feet long. The estimated length of this marine reptile was about 40 feet. Both of these mosasaurs fossils were discovered in the Naiobrara Formation in the state of Kansas.

Hainosaurus was named after the river Haine in Belgium. *Hainosaurus Bernardi* was 40 to 50 feet in length and weighed about 19 tons. Its skull was about five feet long.

Platecarpus or "flat wrist" was a mosasaur species, which grew to a length of 30 feet, and weighed one ton. Specimens of these mosasaurs have been found in the chalk deposits of Kansas, U.S.A. Its powerful paddles and long, flattened tail enabled it to move rapidly through the water. The long jaws contained many sharp coned-shaped teeth and there were teeth in the roof of the mouth as well. These insured that the prey *Platecarpus* had seized upon would not wiggle its way free.

Mary was one of the first people to actually earn a living by collecting and selling fossils. Her customers included many famous paleontologists, as well as the King of Saxony. The latter purchased fossils from her to put in his natural history collection. In 1821 she enjoyed great success in her fossil hunting once again. At this time she discovered a complete skeleton of a new kind of swimming reptile. This creature soon after described by De La Beche and Conybeare received the name "near lizard" or *plesiosaur*. The plesiosaur had a long neck on a short, broad body. Instead of fins, it had four large paddles which enabled it to swim and maneuver in the water. It had a large head with many fine teeth.

Cryptosaurus was a long necked plesiosaur whose jaws contained almost one-hundred small sharp teeth. Elasmosaurus, or "thin-plated lizard" was a giant 40-foot-long sea dragon with an amazingly long neck – one half the size of the entire body. The neck of Elasmosaurus contained about 74 vertebrae. It has been suggested that Elasmosaurus could paddle its way up from the depths of the sea and, by means of its long neck, protrude its head with open jaws into a large school of little fish. Merely by moving its long neck from side-to-side it could gulp down a large amount of fish without having to move its bulky body but very little.

Elasmosaurus had its counterpart on land. The giant sauropod dinosaur, Mamenchisaurus, or "Mammen Creek lizard," found in China, was 72 feet long. Its neck was also one half of the entire body length – 36 feet. This means that Mamenchisaurus could stand off shore in a meandering river and, without having to expend much energy, make a wide, 90 to 100 degree sweep with its long neck and feed for hours on land plants that grew along the river bank.

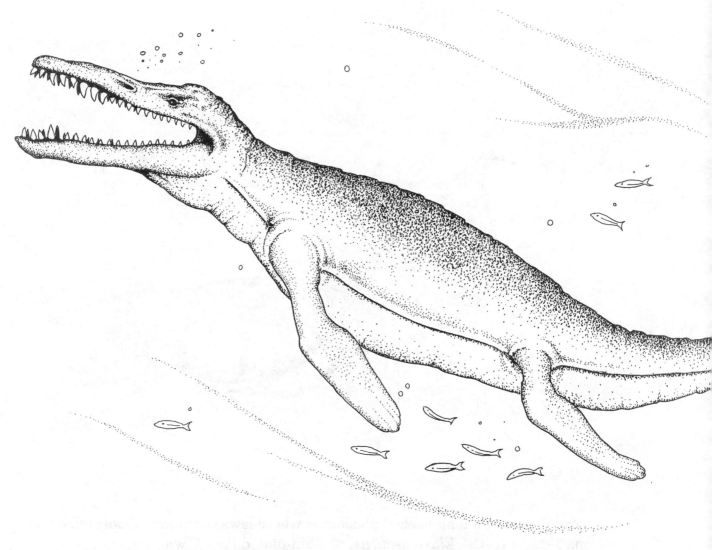

The Sea Dragons, now called pliosaurs were short-necked marine reptiles which lived in the ancient seas. They ranged from approximately 18 to 30 feet in length and possessed a long skull and snout which was at least one-fourth of the total body length. Like the plesiosaurs, the pliosaurs also had powerful paddle-like appendages by which they swam and chased after their prey. The paddles, or flippers, of the pliosaurs had a wing-like appearance and obviously made it possible for these marine giants to swim rapidly and to turn abruptly when chasing after large fish. Some fossilized pliosaur teeth have been found measuring 15 cm in length. In as much as some pliosaur skeletons are found to contain the fossilized remains of their last meal (squid-like creatures), it is evident that they were buried rapidly. This, again, undermines the theory of uniformitarianism and supports the idea of catastrophism and is another physical evidence that the ancient world was overcome by a global flood.

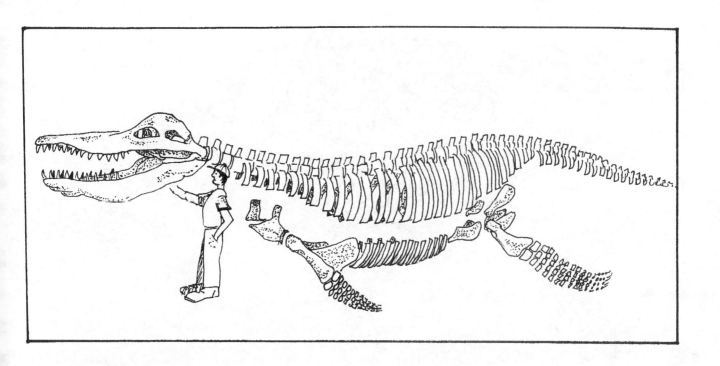

Over the years, artists have sometimes pictured the long-necked, long-tailed plesiosaurs as being perhaps the most fearsome and dragon-like monsters of the ancient seas. Their great size and long serpentine neck surely supports this idea. However, the plesiosaurs, while having many sharp teeth in their mouth, had rather small skulls. The larger forms of marine life and humans (if they had fallen overboard) may have had just as much to fear from the pliosaurs. The longest fossil plesiosaur, *Elasmosaurus* (near lizard), is 40-45 feet in length. The fossilized remains of the pliosaur, *Kronosaurus* (time lizard), shows that it was also about 45 feet in length. However, its skull is an amazing 10 feet long. The short tail of *Kronosaurus* indicates to some researchers that *Kronosaurus* would not have been able to sustain a long chase after its prey. Instead, this large sea monster would have depended on its large front and hind flippers to enable it to lunge after its prey from shorter distances. However, its great size, huge jaws and long, sharp teeth would have made it a most terrible predator.

The most famous pliosaur specimen is *Kronosaurus queenslandicus*. After being dynamited free from its hard, sedimentary casing, it took 20 years to completely remove the skeleton from the various limestone blocks before it could be displayed.

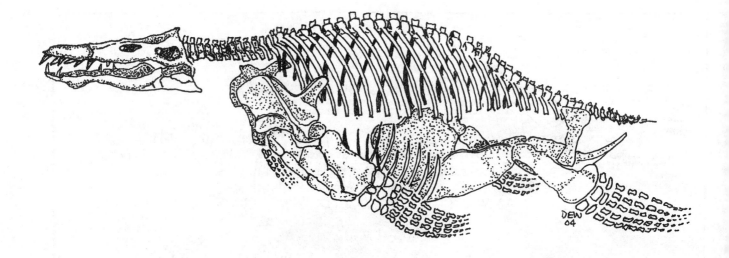

 Liopleurodon or "smooth sided tooth" was one of the giant sea dragons that in the ancient world would have put a great deal of fear into the hearts of any ancient mariners that might have seen one surfacing. This 70 foot long pliosaur, like *Kronosaurus*, had a skull, which was ten feet in length. Its long, large mouth contained many sharp dagger like teeth, the longest of which were located at the end of the snout. Its eyes were on the top of its skull. This has led some researchers to conclude that *Liopleurodon* probably swam in deeper water from where it could spot a variety of larger and smaller fishes swimming above. When it was hungry it would lunge up from the depths, catching its prey unaware. This powerful lunging movement was made possible by the presence of strong flippers and a reinforced rib cage. The reinforced rib cage allowed for the attachment of strong muscles, which made it possible for the flippers to make powerful strokes, lifting the giant upwards. As it shot upwards through the water rapidly its long powerful jaws would bite into the flesh of its prey. Its short, thick neck made it easy for *Liopleurodon*, to rip off large hunks of flesh. It would thrash its neck from side to side violently and tear away the flesh of its prey. Its bite would have been terrible, especially in light of the fact that its teeth were longer than those of the dinosaur *Tyrannosaurus Rex*. The fossil evidence also seems to indicate that this great reptile had an excellent sense of smell, which enabled it to detect small amounts of blood or excrement in the water even from a long distance. Further, its olfactory capacity even made it possible for this creature to detect the direction from which the odor was coming.

It is important to note that the Hebrew word *tannim* is used in the Old
Testament not only for land dragons (dinosaurs) but also for sea dragons. As we
compare the Scriptural references along with other historical accounts, we find that
we are not at all justified in considering the animals to have been fish. Instead, the
various ancient descriptions would seem to compare more favorably with the
marine reptiles of the fossil record: ichthyosaurs, plesiosaurs and mosasaurs.
Perhaps the most notable of these ancient historical accounts is to be found in the
book of Job. In Job 41 we find a rather graphic description of a sea monster
referred to as Leviathan. The specific references to this creature's tongue, nostrils,
neck and very protective scales, strongly indicate that a marine reptile, rather than
a great fish, is here in focus. Again, a review of the fossil record would support the
idea that Leviathan may actually have been a giant sea serpent, or plesiosaur.

Pterosaurs:
The Flying Reptiles

It was Georges Cuvier, the great French anatomist and Creationist, who first identified the pterosaurs as flying animals. He gave the fossil creature earlier described by Collini, the name "Pterodactyl" or "flying finger." Collini had imagined that this strange creature used its wings to propel itself through the water. They were first discovered in Germany. Once the first few discoveries were made, the progress of pterosaur excavations has continued unabated right to the present day. Their remains have now been found on every continent except Antarctica. Pterosaurs were first found in America in the 1870's.

The first American to describe these unusual reptiles was Othniel Marsh, who along with Edward Drinker Cope, was responsible for the discovery and naming of many dinosaurs. Marsh's discovery was made in the state of Kansas. Shortly afterwards, Cope traveled to Kansas and found his own pterosaur, which he described in 1872. In 1876, the American flying reptiles were assigned the name Pteranodon or "toothless flyer" by Marsh. As time went by the Niobrara formation proved to be a happy hunting ground for pterosaur fossils. By 1910, George Eaton, Curator of Osteology and Vertebrate Paleontology at Yale College's Peabody Museum, was able to reference at least 465 separate pterosaur specimens. The Kansas pterosaurs differed from those found in Germany in that they were larger and they had no teeth in their jaws.

In 1971 pterosaurs were first discovered in Brazil, South America. The site is located at Chapada do Araripe. So far 14 new species have been found at this one location. Alltogether, more than 100 species have been found in Brazil.

The word pterosaur means "winged lizard." Perhaps their most striking feature was their unusual crest. It seems apparent that the males and females differed in the size of their crests. In many cases it would also appear that the long crest stretching backward over the head served as an effective counterweight to the long beak. This design probably made it easier for the neck muscles to hold up the head. Some pterosaurs apparently dived into the water in search of fish. In such cases the long crest would have reduced the amount of water resistance.

Pterosaur teeth are all set in individual sockets. In some species the teeth are found only in part of the jaw, while, in others, there are teeth in both the front and back part of the jaw. In yet other species there are no teeth at all. Most of the pterodactyloids had complete sets of teeth. Some pterodactyls had teeth which were thin and closely set together. Some have suggested that they were used as strainers for straining out tiny invertebrates, such as plankton, from the water.

At present we have about 80 fossil imprints of wings to observe. The wings are without feathers and instead, appear to have a skin membrane similar to that of bats. There is an ongoing debate regarding the attachment of pterosaur wings to the body. Some believe that, they were like bats, with the skin membrane attached to the wrist and to the feet or ankles. Others believe they were similar to birds with the wing membrane attached to the mid-body.

At first it was thought that the pterosaurs were only capable of gliding. Recent studies indicate to some researchers that they could fly very well and for long distances. The largest of the pterosaurs are still regarded by many as having used their wings primarily for soaring. Now and then they would have flapped their wings for the purpose of increasing speed, changing directions, and for gaining altitude. The thin, hollow bones of the pterosaurs contribute to the argument that they were capable flyers. The smaller pterosaurs had long tails which were useful in stabilizing them in flight.

Pterosaurs, like ostriches had long hind legs. However, they did not walk flatfooted like humans, but on their toes like dogs. Their hip, knee, and foot joints resemble those of birds. These observations then, lead some to the conclusion that they walked upright. The presence of webbed feet on some pterosaur fossils, indicates that they were probably capable of swimming and of perhaps diving for their prey.

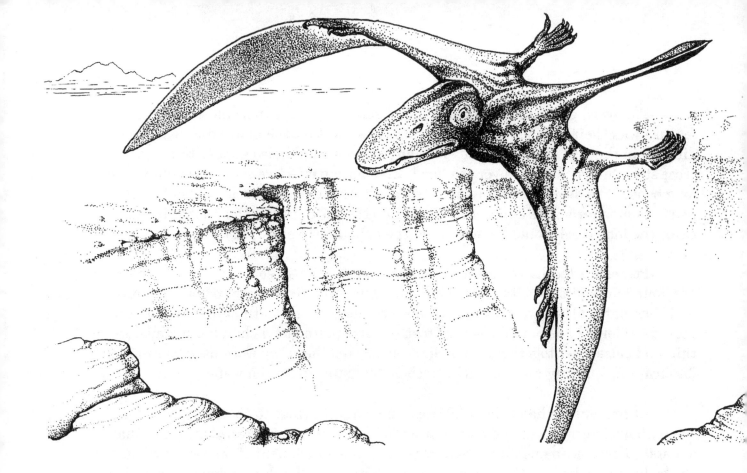

DIMORPHODON MACRONYX

The Christian minister and Professor of Geology, William Buckland, was actually the first to collect the remains of *Dimorphodon*. The fossils were taken from the area in England known as Lime Regis. *Dimorphodon* means "two types of teeth." This good flyer had four large teeth on each side of the upper jaw. Behind them was a row of smaller teeth. The lower jaw had four large front teeth, and behind them on each side of the jaw, there were between thirty and forty small, closely packed teeth. The skull is about eleven and a half inches long. There are openings in the skull which include large eye sockets, nostrils, upper and lower temporal openings and pre-orbital openings. The bone structure of the skull between the holes was very light. *Dimorphodon* was 3.3 feet long and had a wing span of about 4.6 feet. The long tail, which contained thirty vertebrae, was as long as the skull and body together. It's hind legs were long and powerfully built. There were five toes on each of the feet, and the first four of these toes contained claws.

The remains of this flying reptile have been found in association with the remains of the armored dinosaur, *Scelidosaurus*.

PTERODAUSTRO GUINAZUI

This medium sized pterosaur was discovered in Argentina. Its wing span was about 6 feet, and its skull was almost 10 inches long. The lower jaw was long and curved upward, containing perhaps thousands of long, thin teeth. The teeth in the upper jaw were shorter and thicker. The narrow, curved jaw with all of these teeth was certainly an oddity. A variety of reasonable suggestions have been offered as to its use. It seems quite likely that this pterosaur fed on krill and plankton. As it flew low over the water's surface, it would allow its lower jaw to skim. As the water poured into the jaw it would have been forced to the back of the mouth with its contents. Then, when the upper jaw closed, it would force the water out through the closely set teeth, allowing the flying reptile to swallow the food without swallowing the sea water.

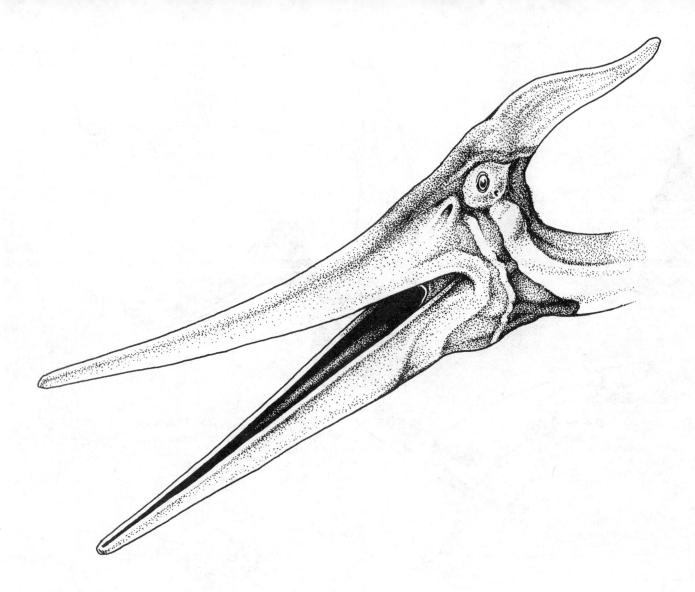

PTERANODON INGENS

Pteranodon was the largest of the flying reptiles. Generally, the members of this group had a wing span of 18 to 20 feet. They had the same unique crests as all the other pterosaurs, however, pteranodon had no teeth. Although a variety of ideas have been given, the exact purpose of these amazing crests is still unknown. One of the most plausible was that it served to cleave the water when pteranodon was diving down for a fish. It is quite possible that the fish they hunted were not always just below the surface.

In general, the fossils of these pterosaurs were found in sediments that, when the reptiles were alive, were a long way from land. Though they were doubtless capable of flapping their wings to gain altitude, it is thought that they were primarily soarers. Their capacity to hunt farther from the shoreline would have given them an advantage not shared by the smaller pterosaurs.

In evolutionary literature these flying reptiles are portrayed as never having lived as contemporaries of man. In fact they are relegated to the prehistoric Mesozoic age which ended 65 million years ago. However, the pterosaurs have been referenced in historic literature, and art in different cultures of the world starting as early as ancient Egypt. In the book of the Hebrew prophet, Isaiah, they are referenced along with other common animals, "The burden of the beasts of the south: into the land of trouble and anguish, from whence come the young and old lion, the viper and fiery, flying serpent..." (Isaiah 30:6). In ancient literature these unusual reptiles are often referred to as winged serpents or as flying dragons. In fact, the Jerusalem Bible translates Isaiah 30:6 as "flying dragons." This is interesting in light of the fact that the Anglo-Saxon Chronicle, which was written more than 1500 years later, references these unusual animals by the same term. "Here dire forewarnings were come over the land of the Northumbrians and sadly terrified the people. There were tremendous lightnings, and fiery dragons were seen flying in the air" (*The Anglo-Saxon Chronicle*, AD 793).

The famous Greek historian, Herodotus, includes in his History, "I went once to a certain place in Arabia, almost exactly opposite the city of Buto, to make inquiries concerning the winged serpents. On my arrival I saw the back-bones and ribs of serpents in such numbers as it is impossible to describe....The winged serpent is shaped like the water-snake. Its wings are not feathered, but resemble very closely those of the bat." (*The History of Herodotus,* Book II, Tudor Publishing Co., New York, 1943, p. 106).

The respected Jewish historian, Josephus, also speaks of flying serpents, "...for when the ground was difficult to be passed over, because of the multitude of serpents, (which it produces in vast numbers, and indeed is singular in some of those productions, which other countries do not breed, and yet such as are worse than others in power and mischief, and an unusual fierceness of sight, some of which ascend out of the ground unseen and also fly in the air, and so come upon men at unawares, and do them a mischief)..." (Josephus, *Complete Works,* Translated by William Whiston, A.M., Kregel Publications --1960, 14th ed. 1977, p. 58).

The Roman poet Lucan also equates these flying creatures with the term dragon,
"You shining Dragons creeping on the earth,
Which fiery Affrick holds with skins like gold,
Yet pestilent by hot infecting breath:
Mounted with wings in th' air we do behold."

Beowolf is the longest and oldest poem written in Old English before the Norman conquest. Beowolf, who developed a reputation for killing a variety of reptilian monsters, was actually himself killed in A.D. 583 by a flying reptile. These creatures were known to the saxons as widfloga or "air-flyers." As Cooper reports, at least two species have been referenced by the Saxons, "...but this particular species of flying reptile, the specimen from Hronesness, was known to them as widfloga, literally a "wide (or far-ranging) flyer", and the description that they have left us fits that of a giant Pteranodon. Interestingly, the Saxons also described this creature as a ligdraca, or fire-dragon, and he is described as fifty feet in length (or perhaps wing-span?)." (Bill Cooper, *After the Flood, New Wine Press* l995 p. 152).

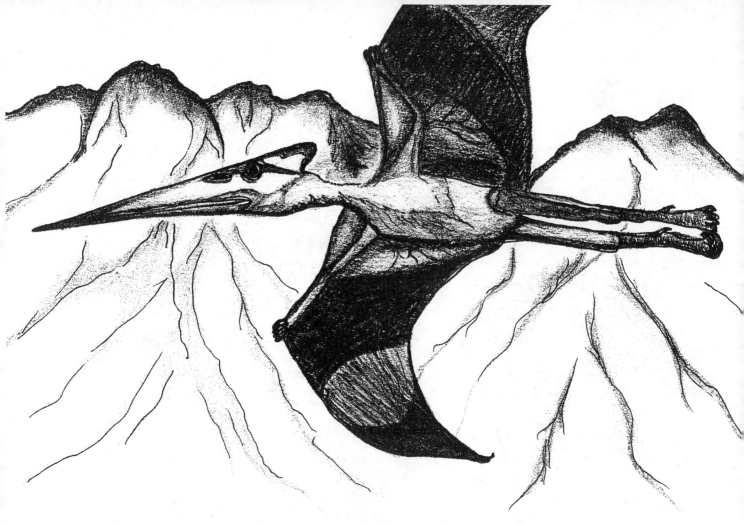

In attempting to name and/or describe these flying reptiles, modern day paleontologists have been at a disadvantage since they have only the fossils to view, and were never able to see the animals alive. The focus of their attention, with regard to naming these unique reptiles, has been on their obvious status as flying creatures. Consequently, they have been given three different names – pterosaurs, meaning "winged lizard;" pterodactyl, meaning "winged finger;" and pteranodon, meaning "winged tooth." Furthermore, modern researchers have focused much attention on the large variety of crests possessed by these flying reptiles.

However, the historic references made by those who saw them alive, emphasize not only their ability to fly, but also another quite different aspect of their appearance – their coloration or sheen. A review of the few historic references already listed in this book should suffice to make the point. In Isaiah 30:6, they are referred to as, "fiery flying serpents." In the Anglo Saxon Chronicle, we read that the, "fiery dragons were seen flying in the air." The Roman poet Lucan pictures these winged creatures as "shining" and as having "skins like gold." In addition to this, in the Anglo Saxon poem Beowulf, these flying reptiles are listed as *ligdraca* (fire dragon) in line 2333, and as *ligegesa* (fire terror) in line 2780.

The impression conveyed by these various writers is not that these animals breathed fire, but that their skin or the hairy covering of their undersides and wings, had a pronounced iridescent quality which, when seen by camp fire or moon light, would have given them a strikingly bright or fiery appearance.

As recently as the early 1900's, elderly folk living in Wales told about the winged serpents in their area, "The woods around Penllin Castle, Glamorgan, had the reputation of being frequented by winged serpents...An aged inhabitant of Penllyne, who died a few years ago, said that in his boyhood the winged serpents were described as very beautiful...When disturbed they glided swiftly, 'sparkling all over,' to their hiding places. When angry, they 'flew over people's heads, with outspread wings bright, and sometimes with eyes too, like the feathers in a peacock's tail.'" (Trevelyan, M. 1909, *Folk-Lore and Folk Stories of Wales*) cit. Simpson, J. British Dragons. B.T. Batsford Ltd. London, 1980)

It is most interesting in this regard to note that the Hebrew word for these peculiar reptilian creatures is not the word *tannin*, which in the Scriptures has been appropriately translated as dragon and sea dragon. Instead, the Hebrew word for the flying reptiles is the word *seraph*, from which we have our word seraphim. These unique angelic creatures are distinguished by their possession of wings (Isaiah 6:2). However, the meaning of the word *seraph* is "burning". Apparently, to the Old Testament writer, the bright, iridescent appearance of these reptiles justified the use of the Hebrew word *seraph* as an appropriate name.

Dinosaur Discoveries

Noah's ark contained representatives of all of the air-breathing species in the animal kingdom. However, since the atmosphere, climate and environment of the new world were vastly different from that of the old, it would not be unreasonable to expect that some species would do better than others. The one notable group which we might expect to have a greater challenge adjusting to and surviving in the new world was the dinosaur. Probably, the larger of the dinosaurs would have been first to move toward extinction. The smaller ones would have endured for a longer period of time.

Among the first generations of people after the Flood, dinosaurs would have appeared as common as dogs and sheep. As the new conditions began to affect the dinosaurs adversely, however, an increasing number of their kind would find it difficult to cope with the natural adversities. Generation by generation, one dinosaur kind after another would have become extinct. Thus, as history progressed from the time of the Flood, fewer and fewer people would have the experience of seeing, first-hand, these unusual creatures. In some parts of the world they would be common, while in other areas, where the weather was frequently inclement, their kind was never seen at all. In these areas, they would be known only by their inclusion in the storytelling hour around campfires. These stories would have been considered quite valid in the same way that we attach credence to the deer or bear stories told to us today by relatives and friends.

For awhile, even the infrequent observation of dinosaur herds or individuals served to validate all dinosaur stories. Besides the secular accounts, the dinosaur or dragon is mentioned specifically in the book of Job and in other Scriptures. This indicates that in certain areas of the world, where the vegetation and climate was appropriate, the dinosaurs were alive and doing well.

Scripture verifies their existence as late as 400 B.C. The secular accounts record the existence of dragons on the earth up to approximately 1200 A.D. Eventually, however, the dinosaurs seemed to have disappeared altogether. At last mankind was left with only stories. The descendants of each family had to accept the accounts of dragons on faith.

In many of the countries of the world, these unusual reptiles were known as dragons. As time went by, storytellers subtracted from and added to the known information. Eventually, descriptions of the dragons bore less and less resemblance to the real thing. After so many years, fewer and fewer people believed in the old tales. Finally, when people in modern times came across dinosaur fossils they were not inclined to link these fossils to the dragon.

Nevertheless, such daring explorers as Columbus were warned that, if they ventured too far out to sea, they would be devoured by giant sea monsters. Such ideas are remnants of the original stories of the real dinosaurs. Generally speaking, however, by the time of Columbus both the dragons and the knowledge of them had become extinct. Giant fossil bones were assumed to be from elephants or some other large animal. Thus, in the modern era, when science began to come into its own, the first discoverers of the dragons were at a loss to identify what they had found.

One of the first records which we have of someone finding a dinosaur bone was in 1677. At that time, Robert Plot, an Oxford University Professor, included a drawing of a dinosaur bone in his book, *The Natural History of Oxfordshire*. Although he drew and described it well, Plot was at a loss to identify the creature from which the bone had come. At first, he suggested that it might have been from an elephant brought to Britain by the Roman government centuries earlier. Later, after having been able to observe an elephant, he concluded that it must have come from a giant human.

WILLIAM BUCKLAND

In the early 1800's there were a number of intellectuals who had become fond of collecting fossils. It was good exercise and provided a measure of intrigue. The fossils spoke of an ancient age, thus, each one could be considered as a mysterious link between the modern world and the First World.

By 1818, William Buckland, an Anglican priest and professor of Geology at Oxford, had obtained a small collection of fossils. Buckland was a Creationist who was highly regarded for his scholarly work at the university. He shared his fossils with Georges Cuvier, who was later to be considered the father of comparative anatomy. Both men had found the theory of evolution to be scientifically untenable. Although they believed the Bible, they were not able to relate these fossil bones to the giant creatures mentioned in Job and Psalms. Due to the size of the bones, however, they both recognized that it must have come from a very large animal indeed. They were observing limb bones, ribs, vertebrae and a jaw bone with long, knife-like teeth. These bones were found at Stonefield, a small quarrying village near Oxford. Finally, at Cuvier's bidding, Buckland published a description of these findings in 1824. By that time he had come to the conclusion the bones were reptilian. Consequently, he named it *Megalosaurus* but customarily referred to it as "the great fossil lizard of Stonesfield."

GIDEON MANTELL

One day in 1822, a country doctor named Gideon Mantell, accompanied by his wife Mary Ann, went to visit a patient at Lewes in Sussex, England. While the doctor visited with the patient, Mary Ann went for a walk. Soon she came across a large fossil tooth amidst a pile of rocks. Shortly thereafter, she showed it to her husband, who, besides being a medical doctor, was also an amateur paleontologist. He was enthusiastic about her find, and suspected it to be from a very unusual animal. He set about sharing it with some of his educated friends, asking their opinions.

Dr. Mantell took the tooth to a meeting of the Geological Society in London, where he showed it to Buckland, Conybeare and others. Their conclusion was that it was of no significant interest. Mantell then sent the tooth to Baron Cuvier in Paris, who deduced that it must have come from an ancient rhinoceros. Only a friend of Mantell's, Dr. Walliston, supported the opinion that Mantell had found the tooth of an unknown herbivorous reptile.

The logistical problem was that the tooth had been found in strata considered to be too old for mammals, and yet the tooth showed that it was worn from use. Mantell knew of no living reptile which masticated its food. The only other option was to consider it from some giant, very ancient, and yet unknown reptile.

Mantell learned that the gravel in which the tooth had been found had originally come from quarries in the Cuckfield area of the Tilgate Forest. He continued his search there, where he came upon more teeth and bones belonging to the same creature, including some metacarpal bones. These metacarpals he forwarded to Paris, to Cuvier, who identified them as belonging to an ancient hippopotamus.

At last, Mantell decided to take his fossil finds to the Hunterian Museum at the Royal College of Surgeons in London. There he went about comparing his finds with the many teeth and skeletal parts in the museum's large collection. This was a time-consuming project which wore on fruitlessly through the day. Finally, at the end of the day, he fell into conversation with a student by the name of Stutchbury. He shared his plight and showed the teeth to his new acquaintance. This was a critical moment in the discovery of dinosaurs. The young Stutchbury was then studying the Iguana lizard of Central America. He was almost certain that Mantell's fossil teeth resembled those of the Iguana. He was able to show Dr. Mantell some Iguana teeth for comparison. The similarities were striking. Dr. Mantell was now even more confident that his teeth were from a giant and now extinct reptile.

Mantell's paper on the subject was published in the *Philosophical Transactions* of the Royal Society of London in 1825. Bearing in mind the Iguana of Central America, he had named the creature *Iguanodon*, meaning "iguana tooth."

Several years later, in 1833, the front half of another dinosaur skeleton was discovered in the Tilgate Forest area of Sussex, England. Dr. Mantell also named and described the creature. *Hylaeosaurus* was the third dinosaur to be named and described in modern times. Its name means "woodland reptile" in reference to the area in which it was found.

RICHARD OWEN

Richard Owen was a most extraordinary man. He was not content to allow one area of science to occupy all of his attention. Besides practicing medicine, he was able to make significant contributions to other disciplines. In 1836, he was appointed as Huntarian Professor in the Royal College of Surgeons. Soon he began to distinguish himself as a proficient anatomist. In 1849 he succeeded William Clift as the Conservator of the Royal College of Surgeons.

His learning and reputation increased. In 1856, he obtained the position of Superintendent of the Natural History division of the British Museum. His knowledge and interest in natural history would not allow him to be content with the artifacts of natural history crowded into a small section of a larger museum. He envisioned a separate museum, one totally devoted to natural history, and, in time, lived to see it come to pass.

The science of comparative anatomy, which had been founded by Cuvier, was now carried on in England by Owen. In fact, his achievements in this area have caused him to be remembered as England's pioneer anatomist and paleontologist. Actually, he had had the opportunity to meet Cuvier in Paris. Their meeting had lasting effects on Owen, who was at that time a budding young anatomist. It is interesting to note that both of these men were Creationists and believed that the earth's sedimentary layers were deposited by the world-wide Flood mentioned in Genesis.

Owen soon gained a substantial reputation and was regarded, even as a young man, as a leader in British science. Many came to him for his opinion on a variety of questions dealing with anatomy and paleontology. Along the way, he became a personal friend of Queen Victoria. He was often a guest at the palace, where he gave fascinating lectures on nature to her and her large family.

Among his many achievements is the identification of the reptilian kind now known as dinosaurs, as being quite distinct from the reptiles which we see today. He had described a number of these reptiles, and was well aware of those which had been excavated and described by others. By 1841, nine genera of giant reptiles were known to Owen and other paleontologists. The ones which Owen studied in particular detail were *Iguanodon*, *Megalosaurus* and *Hylaeosaurus*.

Over the years, he had dissected a number of reptiles which had died at the Regents Park Zoo in London. Consequently, he began to realize that the anatomy of the fossil reptiles was significantly different from that of the modern reptiles. He concluded that the fossil reptiles could not be placed in the families or even the orders under which modern reptiles were classified. He felt that reptiles such as *Iguanodon* and *Megalosaurus* belonged in a special order of their own. He conceived of them not merely as giant reptiles, but as terrible lizards or "dinosauria". This name he proposed at the meeting of the British Association for the Advancement of Science in 1841. It was published in 1842 in the *Proceedings of the British Association for the Advancement of Science*.

In 1859, Darwin's *Origin of the Species* was published. As a physician, anatomist and paleontologist, Owen could not see the viability of evolution in any spectrum of science with which he dealt. He was confident that the earth had been created, and that the fossils and sedimentary layers were the direct results of a world-wide deluge. He was totally opposed to the uniformitarian concept of geology, and would not change his opinion to appease the new scholasticism. He maintained this position to the end of his life. As a result, despite his great accomplishments, he began to be regarded as an "anti-progressive" by the new school of younger geologists who readily embraced the evolutionary theory.

In the early 1800's, unusual tracks were noticed by travelers and settlers in the Connecticut River Valley. Many of the prints were three-toed and quite large. They came to be popularly referred to as the tracks of Noah's ravens. Eventually, Edward Hitchcock, Professor of Natural Theology and Geology at Amherst College, began a life-long study of these tracks. He spent many summers walking back and forth across the Connecticut River Valley looking for more of them. He was quite successful in finding them; in fact, his collection became so large and extensive that Amherst College built a museum to house a large number of these specimens.

In addition to this, in 1858, the state of Massachusetts published a large volume providing information on the tracks. It was entitled *Ichnology of New England*. Among the kinds of tracks which the author identifies are those of lizards, turtles and amphibians. The three-toed tracks were, in Hitchcock's opinion, those of giant birds. Modern opinion considers these to be the tracks of dinosaurs, although there is yet considerable debate as to which dinosaurs the tracks belong. The dinosaurs with which they have theoretically been associated are: *Eubrontes, Anchisauripus, Grallator* and *Sauropus*.

JOSEPH LEIDY

Dr. Joseph Leidy was the professor of anatomy at the medical school of the University of Pennsylvania. Early in his career, he became associated with the Academy of Natural Sciences in Philadelphia. In 1855, he received some fossil teeth from Ferdinand Hayden, who was one of the first scientific explorers of the territory west of the Mississippi. In March 1856, Dr. Leidy published a description of these teeth which had been found in Montana. He considered some of the fossils to be from a dinosaur. A close study of some of the teeth indicated that the dinosaur was herbivorous and was probably related to *Iguanodon*. He gave the creature the name *Trachodon*, but it is now commonly known as *Anatosaurus*.

Dr. Leidy's conclusions were admittedly tentative since the evidence was so scant. Two years later, however, he obtained evidence that allowed him to be more confident of his conclusions. In 1858, a Mr. Hopkins, a farmer in Haddonfield, New Jersey, was talking to his friend Mr. William P. Foulke, about the large fossil bones he and his workers had found while involved in a digging operation 20 years earlier. Foulke, a resident of Philadelphia who was vacationing in Haddonfield, was intensely interested in the find. Consequently, Mr. Hopkins gave him permission to attempt to locate and dig up the fossils. After much searching, Foulke's hired workers finally came across the old pit where the bones had previously been discovered. Soon, Dr. Leidy was apprised of the discovery, and came immediately to the site. After much study and observation of the bones, Leidy proposed the name of *Hadrosaurus* in December of 1858. He was convinced that this dinosaur, too, was related to *Iguanodon*. *Trachodon* had consisted of only a few teeth. The newly discovered *Hadrosaurus*, on the other hand, consisted of 9 teeth, part of the lower jaw, 28 vertebrae, bones of the hind feet and forelimbs, and most importantly, bones of the pelvis.

Leidy's published description of *Hadrosaurus* suggested that the dinosaur stood upright, much in the fashion of a kangaroo. Thus, Dr. Leidy was able to establish the fact that dinosaurs had been as much a part of animal life in North America as they had in Europe. Leidy was also the first scientist to place a bipedal dinosaur in its correct posture.

OTHNIEL CHARLES MARSH

Othniel C. Marsh, who began life as a farm boy, was able to receive an excellent education primarily by means of financial contributions from a wealthy uncle. After graduating from Yale, he was afforded a lengthy study trip to Europe, where he was able to visit many museums and further his academic studies.

In 1865, he became Professor of Paleontology at Yale. He was to be the curator of the museum's fossil collection, and since he had no teaching duties, he was able to devote himself entirely to the study of fossils. Even in this, his income came by way of his uncle. He soon became a highly respected authority in the area of paleontology. Much of his renown was due to his development of the large fossil collection at the Yale Museum.

He acted as the first vertebrate paleontologist for the U.S. Geological Survey for ten years and served as president of the National Academy of Sciences for twelve years. As a result of his connections at Yale, the U.S. Geological Survey and the National Academy of Sciences, Marsh was able to work with an on-going and liberal budget in his search for the dinosaurs.

EDWARD DRINKER COPE

Edward D. Cope had a strong interest in nature, even as a child. Cope's first scientific paper was published at the age of 18; Marsh's first was not published until he was 30. As a young man, Cope was able to greatly increase his knowledge of living and fossil animals while studying in Europe. Near the end of the American Civil War, he returned from Europe, becoming a member of the faculty of Haverford College. Soon thereafter, he moved to Haddonfield, New Jersey where he was able to pursue his studies at full throttle.

In time he became widely acknowledged as an expert in fossil vertebrate paleontology as well as in modern fishes, amphibians and reptiles. He has come to be regarded as the founder of the science of vertebrate paleontology in North America. He became an excellent researcher and prodigious writer. By the end of his life, his scientific publications numbered about 1,400. In contrast, even though Marsh had greater financial resources for fossil collecting, his publications numbered only 270.

At the age of 35, Cope inherited a fortune from his father, but poor investments eventually eliminated this advantage. In the end, it was necessary for him to live off a professor's salary at the University of Pennsylvania.

Cope's eminence in the world of science came more after his death than during his life. The lone honor for his many achievements was given to him toward the end of his life when he was elected President of the American Association for the Advancement of Science.

THE BONE WARS

Cope and Marsh began a working relationship under reasonably friendly terms in 1868. Within a year, however, they had begun a personal feud which was to continue for the rest of their lives.

In 1877, Arthur Lakes and O.W. Lucas, two schoolmasters, found some fossil bones near Morrison, Colorado. Since both Cope and Marsh were well-known as dinosaur paleontologists, specimens were sent to each of them by the two men who were unaware of the antagonism. Marsh, through clever manipulation, soon obtained possession of all the fossils in this discovery, much to Cope's consternation.

Then, Mr. Lucas came across some gigantic bones near Canyon City, Colorado. These were sent to Cope, which put him temporarily at an advantage, for the Canyon City fossils were of greater size and the collection was more complete than those found in the Morrison location.

Soon afterwards, it was Marsh's turn to gain the upper hand. He received a letter from two men from the Union Pacific Railroad, telling of the gigantic bones they had discovered at Como Bluffs, Wyoming. Marsh sent his assistant, Samuel Williston, to investigate the discovery. After observing the site, Williston sent a glowing report of the discovery to Marsh, stating that the fossil material extended for seven miles and that it would be relatively easy to excavate. After Dr. Marsh concluded a financial deal with the discoverers, W.E. Carlin and W.H. Reed, work began on the excavations. The work at Como Bluffs was done in utmost secrecy lest Cope find out and send in his own collectors. From 1877 to 1883, the work continued, resulting in an enormous amount of fossil material being sent to Marsh.

The centennial year of the U.S. proved to be a most disastrous one for a famous American general, George Armstrong Custer. That was the year Sitting Bull and the Indians destroyed the large cavalry patrol under Custer's command at the Little

Bighorn. Shortly after this unfortunate American defeat, Edward Cope came west to join a famous dinosaur hunter, Charles Sternberg.

When he arrived in Helena, Montana, he found a city filled with anxiety over the recent massacre. Cope received dire warnings against venturing into Sioux territory at such a perilous time. Nevertheless, intrepid man that he was, he hired a cook and a scout to accompany him and his two assistants and off they went.

En route, they did encounter a number of Indians, none of which proved to be dangerous. Cope went out of his way to be friendly, even to the point of removing his false teeth and snapping them back into his mouth. This magical feat so awed the Indians that they insisted it be performed several times.

When Cope and his crew reached the Judith River formation, they began a summer of difficult and laborious work. Up and down the steep cliffs they traversed, quenching their thirst in the hot summer with water that was thoroughly repugnant to the taste.

Though the work was hard, the payoff was encouraging. In this dig they found *Monoclonius* and the remains of a variety of hadrosaurs. At summer's end, they had a wagon load of valuable material to bring home. The perils, however, were not yet fully past. As expected, Sitting Bull and his warriors were in the process of retreating from the south at that time. Cope's scout came across their camp during one of his outings. Later that day, the scout and the cook abandoned the expedition, leaving Cope, Sternberg and his companion, Issacs to manage the wagon by themselves. The plan was to take the fossils by wagon to the steamboat dock downstream. However, this mission now required haste, for having stayed so long there was now only one more steamboat scheduled that season.

Hour by hour, the small crew struggled to get the wagon down the steep cliffs and then down the river to the dock. Sore and exhausted, they managed to arrive just in time to catch that last steamboat. This ended Cope's explorations in Montana until 1896, four years before his death.

The discovery which went far to enhance the reputation of Othniel Marsh was that of the horned dinosaurs. No one had ever conceived of such a creature prior to that time, and even Marsh considered the first pair of horns sent to him to be from an extinct bison. These horns came by way of Whitman Cross, a government geologist working in the Denver beds. Later on, in 1888, Marsh received a letter from a certain John Hatcher who was on his way back to the east coast. Hatcher told of his discovery of a large horn attached to a skull. Soon after, the horn was sent to Marsh, who found it to be quite similar to the first pair. At this point, he began to have misgivings about his identification of the first set of horns.

In short order, Hatcher was asked to retrieve the skull and send it to Marsh in New Haven. Marsh found the skull to be an astonishing specimen, weighing approximately one ton. They had truly found something remarkable.

In the years to follow, Hatcher became well-known in scientific circles for his association with the horned dinosaurs. By 1892, he had collected the fossils of 50 horned dinosaurs. The skulls of some of these giants weighed as much as 3 1/2 tons.

The bone wars between Marsh and Cope were perhaps an amusing display of egocentricity. However, the fruit of their rivalry produced for the world of science a new and more complete vista of the strange and awesome world of the dinosaurs.

Prior to their efforts, only 9 dinosaurs had been found in North America. By the time their long and bitter feud had ended, 136 more species had been added to that number.

BELGIUM

In 1878, while Marsh and Cope were trying to outdo one another, a famous dinosaur discovery was being made in Belgium in a quiet and less acrimonious manner. These bones were found by coal miners in a mine near Bernissart, Belgium. One of the most amazing things about this discovery is that the skeletons were found over 1000 feet below the surface of the earth. In a space of three years, 31 nearly complete skeletons were recovered and subsequently identified as *Iguanodon*. The company which owned the Fosse Ste-Barbe mine near Bernissart had dispatched a group of miners to develop a new and deeper gallery. At a depth of 1046 feet, they came upon a cache of fossil bones. Due to the dim light in the narrow tunnel, the miners destroyed virtually an entire skeleton before they realized what kind of material they were digging through.

The workers forwarded word to the director of the mine, who quickly informed the Royal Belgian Museum of Natural History in Brussels of the discovery. The museum sent P.J. van Deneden, a well-known Belgian paleontologist, to the mine. It did not take him long to discern that the bones belonged to a species of Iguanodon, and that there was a very large number of them.

The more the workers surveyed the scene, the more dinosaurs they realized lay buried there. Finally, Mr. Gustave Arnould, the mine's chief engineer, requested that expert technical help be made available for a proper and safe excavation. The man who took over the supervision of the excavation was Mr. De Pauw, who was in charge of the museum's laboratory. For the next three years, he labored with the miners and excavators in the tedious and somewhat dangerous work of excavating dinosaur skeletons located over 1000 feet below the surface of the earth.

Eventually, a parallel tunnel was dug 150 feet below the first. To their utter amazement, they found more dinosaur fossils. This amazing fossil graveyard had the unique characteristic of protruding vertically through more than 100 feet of coal. This vertical configuration argues strongly against the uniformitarian explanation that the dinosaurs had all wandered into a dense marsh, gotten bogged down, and then over millions of years, fossilized. Dinosaurs buried in a bog would of necessity be found in a horizontal plane. In such a case, they would be found side by side, rather than on top of one another.

Another unusual feature of this find was that the bones were not contained within the regular stratified bed of the coal mines. Instead, they had been deposited in unstratified clay. De Pauw's explanation of this phenomenon is as follows: The coal deposit formed over millions of years, during which time a deep ravine developed. Many *Iguanodons* must have fallen into the ravine. Subsequent flood waters washed mud and sedimentary material into the ravine, covering the dinosaurs.

It is conceivable, though not very probable, that one dinosaur could have fallen into the ravine. It is even less probable that a second dinosaur suffered the same fate, but to assume that 31 *Iguanodons* would all be so careless and clumsy as to fall into the same ravine is, certainly, not the most reasonable explanation.

Modern scientific experimentation has demonstrated that coal can be formed quite rapidly. On the other hand, we know that organisms cannot become fossilized over long periods of time due to the problems of oxidation and decomposition.

In light of these facts, we are warranted to make the suggestion that the dinosaurs and the massive amounts of vegetation which became coal are victims of the same catastrophe. The vegetation had been ripped away and carried off by an ever-increasing volume of water.

The vegetation which preceded the helpless dinosaurs eventually began to accumulate en masse at the point of deposition. The dinosaurs and the sedimentary material over which they were traversing soon came to rest against the growing underwater wall of vegetation. However, the masses of vegetation which followed them, by virtue of its weight and the velocity of the water, caused the dinosaur herd to be squeezed into a vertical column which thereafter ensured rapid fossilization.

It was a long and arduous task to get the dinosaurs out of their inconvenient burial ground, deep within the mine. De Pauw and the workers did a praiseworthy job in their excavations. During their progress, the crews were careful to maintain surveys and measurements of the locations of each of the fossil pieces so that they could be properly assembled when they were taken back to the museum. Whole blocks of coal shale were taken out and numbered. This made it easier for the paleontologists to connect the related pieces during the reconstruction.

The first skeleton was mounted in 1883, but it took about 25 years before all the reconstructions were finally complete. In the meantime, the dinosaur display was open for public viewing at the famous Chapel St. Georges in Brussels. Today, at the Brussels Museum, visitors may see eleven fully erect skeletons and 20 other complete and partial reconstructions nearby.

AMERICAN MUSEUM OF NATURAL HISTORY

In the summer of 1897, Barnum Brown and Walter Granger of the Museum of Natural History returned to the famous Como Bluffs dinosaur site first worked by Marsh and Cope. Henry Fairfield Osborn, who had come to the museum in 1891, had desired material for his research in fossil vertebrae. This expedition was an extension of his research program. Since Osborn had also developed a keen interest in dinosaurs along the way, Marsh's happy hunting grounds in Wyoming seemed a propitious site for fulfilling his objectives.

Osborn knew that large dinosaur skeletons would do much to gain public interest in the museum. This, in turn, would generate philanthropic contributions and significantly enhance the prestige and importance of the museum.

The first crew set out in 1897 with high hopes. The team consisted of Barnum Brown, Walter Granger, Dr. Wortman and H. W. Menke along with some assistants. After much searching, they found that Marsh's men had taken away all the fossils that lay close to the surface. Consequently, it took weeks for the crew to remove tons of overburden before they were able to get to untouched material. They even went to the trouble of sending the huge quantity of overburden back to the museum in hopes that the workers there might sift through it and find valuable bones. It was however, a vain pursuit. The material was devoid of anything significant.

Finally, Osborn himself came to visit the site of excavation. One day, he and Barnum Brown went off on a little hunt along the bluff. It proved to be a profitable foray, because they soon came across the fossil of a dinosaur. Encouraged by this, Wortman went off on a search of his own. His quest also ended successfully in the discovery of yet another dinosaur. The excavation of these two specimens occupied the crew for the remainder of the summer.

The following summer the crew, with a new member, Albert Thompson, returned to the Bluffs. Their enthusiasm, however, was diminished as the days went by, for they had no success in finding the desired treasures. At last, it was decided to move northward to the Medicine Bow anticline to establish a new camp.

Years before, a shepherd in this area had come across a graveyard of dinosaur bones. When the crew arrived they found that the enterprising shepherd had constructed an entire cabin of dinosaur bones. The new find, later referred to as "Bone Cabin Quarry," had been handed to them on a silver platter. Years of rainy weather had eroded away the covering sediments so that large fragments of fossils could easily be seen. The more they dug, the more they found. All summer and autumn they labored getting the fossils out of the ground and ready for the trip back to New York. The load had to be taken back in two freight cars provided by J.P. Morgan--160,000 pounds at seasons end. Then, for the next seven years, crews from the American Museum of Natural History continued the excavations.

During these years, branch excavations were tried to see what might be found in adjacent areas. About five miles to the south of Bone Cabin Quarry, a new camp was set up. There the men found a brontosaur skeleton. When the teams returned in 1901, it was assumed that things were drawing to a close in the area. However, much to their delight and surprise, they came upon yet another bonanza that Granger considered the most valuable find of all. Then, as if that wasn't enough, later in the year Bill Reed showed up with news of a new discovery. (This was the Bill Reed who about twenty five years earlier had informed Marsh of the Como Bluff fossil find.) After developing a contract of sorts with the Museum through Walter

Granger, he led the team into the new site, called Quarry R. This was about fourteen miles from Bone Cabin. The next summer the excavators began in earnest to work the site. In 1902, 1903 and 1905 the workers excavated at both locations with wonderful results.

They had now reached the end of the line, but what a long and prosperous one it had been. During those years of plenty the workers had collected 483 dinosaur bones and sent back 160,000 pounds of material for further study.

WALTER GRANGER

In 1890, the young Walter Granger began his long association with the American Museum of Natural History in a most humble station. Though he was able to dabble a bit in the taxidermy department, his primary function lay in the realm of custodial services. When various creatures died in the Central Park Zoo, they were often taken to the museum where they were stuffed. In this way, they were preserved for the benefit of the many wildlife observers who regularly visited the Museum. Walter Granger's humble part in this activity was to skin and preserve the birds. Then, little by little, his responsibilities grew. He was a good observer, a good worker and a quick learner of tasks that were important to Museum operations. We have already mentioned in some detail his participation in the excavations which took place at Como Bluff years later. In fact, he took complete charge of the work from the Museum in Pittsburg.

Beginning in 1902, however, he shifted his attention and energies to the study of mammalian life. In this work he also distinguished himself and was extremely influential. His return to the dinosaurs came in April of 1922 when he left to be second in command under Roy Chapman Andrews in the expedition to Central Asia.

BARNUM BROWN

In 1902, Barnum Brown left Como Bluffs for the badlands of Montana. Though it took a long time to reach the location where they estimated the dinosaur fossils to be, it did not take them long to locate the dinosaur fossils once they were in the territory.

In what is known as the Hell Creek formation, they came upon a large and well preserved *Tyrannosaurus* skeleton. However, excavating the huge skeleton was not an easy task. The sandstone bed in which the fossil had been imbedded was extremely hard. Finally, it became necessary for the crew to cut it into blocks for shipping back to the museum. One of these blocks weighed about 4000 pounds, and it took two summers of work just to get this one giant skeleton out of the earth and on its way to the museum. During the next several years of digging a variety of dinosaurs were discovered, including a second *Tyrannosaurus* and some duckbill skeletons.

After the 1908 season, Dr. Brown decided to look elsewhere for dinosaurs. Eventually, he found his way to the Red Deer River in Alberta, Canada. Earlier reports had indicated that this area might well be a profitable location in the search for the giant reptile fossils. Dr. Brown soon came to the conclusion that the best way to observe the cliffs of the river would be by boat. Consequently, he had a very special boat built for this purpose--a flat bottom barge. This provided the room for hauling away their treasures once they found them.

This canyon represents one of the many run-off rivulets or streams by means of which the world-wide Flood waters of Noah's day fled down and outward to lower elevations at the end of the flood year. The layers of sedimentary deposits through which it cut had not yet had time to completely harden. Thus, the quantity of water now flowing downward to the lowlands was able to cut through the sedimentary layers with little difficulty. The Red Deer River is a thin and often slow-moving reminder of the great waters which once developed the canyon.

It was not long into their boat trip before the hunting party spotted fossils protruding out of the cliffs. Then, day after day, they located one dinosaur after another. In one area they found a 32-foot *Saurolophus*. By the time they had finished at that site, they had excavated about 100 individual dinosaurs.

The wonderful successes of this expedition, however, almost brought about a negative end to the whole story. Once the Canadians found out about the success of the American expeditions, they realized that all of this fossil material was going back to decorate and popularize American museums. This problem began to cause quite an uproar. There were some who tried to get the Canadian government to refuse the Americans permission to excavate along the Red Deer River in the Canadian territory. In the end, the decision was made not to prohibit the Americans from excavating, but instead, it was decided that Canadian scientists would take advantage of the opportunities which lay before them.

Soon they had their own representatives boating up and down the river in search of dinosaur fossils. The Canadian team was unusual in that it consisted primarily of one family--the Sternbergs. Charles Sternberg and his three sons soon went about their task with gusto.

So, for the next few years, the two rival teams--the Americans and the Canadians--went up and down the river gathering dinosaur fossils. Thankfully, there was an abundance of fossils and this prevented the rivalry from ever becoming hostile. The Sternberg's collection included horned dinosaurs, armored dinosaurs and duckbills.

Barnum Brown's work continued there until 1915. The Sternbergs ended their main work shortly thereafter. Two of the sons, however, continued for many years searching for and finding a variety of fossils to further enrich the collection already developing in the Canadian museums. Barnum Brown was with the American Museum for 60 years. As an individual, he has probably found more dinosaurs than anyone else in the history of dinosaur discoverers.

ANDREW CARNEGIE

Andrew Carnegie's family came to America from Scotland when he was twelve years old. By age seventeen, he had taught himself to be a telegraph operator. It was as a telegraph operator that he got a job for the Pennsylvania Railroad. He was promoted regularly, and soon became division superintendent.

After a trip to Europe, he realized the need for steel in modern industries would increase in the future. In 1873, he and several partners built a steel mill near Pittsburgh which was the most modern of its day. The mill became quite successful, and, in time, Carnegie was able to buy out one of his chief competitors. In 1892, he combined three of his business ventures and created the Carnegie Steel Company. By the time he retired, he was worth $500 million and was considered to be the richest man in the world.

During the course of his long and successful career, he made generous contributions to a variety of worthy causes--one of which had to do with the founding of a nationally famous museum in Pittsburgh.

As the Carnegie Museum began to develop, Carnegie himself took a keen interest in the search for dinosaurs. In time, millions of dollars of Carnegie money would be used in dinosaur excavations.

In 1908, Earl Douglass, an employee of Carnegie's museum, discovered a *Diplodocus* femur in the Green River/Split Mountain Gorge area of Utah. Then, in 1909, he made a momentous discovery of fossil material in the Morrison formation near Vernal, Utah. The amount of bones taken from this location is considered to be unequalled in the history of dinosaur excavations. In fact, there are still crates from this find that lay unpacked in the Carnegie Museum today. Among the dinosaur specimens unearthed here were *Apatosaurus*, *Diplodocus*, *Camptosaurus*, *Stegosaurus* and *Allosaurus*.

One of the giant specimens which Dr. Holland, Director of the Carnegie Museum, described was given the name *Diplodocus-carnegie*. Mr. Carnegie appreciated the name and admired the skeleton so much that he decided to share it. He insisted on casts being made of the *Diplodocus* skeleton so that it could be sent to other museums. This complex task took much time and an enormous amount of money. Carnegie, who was no skinflint in such matters, saw it through to the end. Eventually, entire Diplodocus skeletons, big enough to fill a barn, were sent to museums in Britain, France, Germany, Austria, Argentina and Mexico. Between the years 1898 and 1905, Mr. Carnegie spent about $25 million on his fossil collecting expeditions.

EARL DOUGLASS

Earl Douglass was in Utah collecting fossil mammals for the Carnegie Museum when Dr. Holland, the museum's director, came for a visit. When they learned the area they were near had good potential for yielding dinosaur fossils, they both set about to see what they could find.

Eventually, Douglass came upon a dinosaur thigh bone in a ravine. This was the appetizer that brought him back the following season for an all-out hunt for dinosaurs. In mid-August, after some discouraging and fruitless weeks of searching, he came upon some fragments of bone in a gully. Further searching in the immediate area revealed eight dinosaur tail vertebrae in articulation. The more Douglass worked here, the more he realized that it was highly probable that a whole skeleton would be found along with the tail. Confident he had found a beautiful specimen, he wrote Dr. Holland of his discovery and soon local citizenry were hired and trained to facilitate the excavation.

In time, Earl Douglass was joined by his wife and year old baby. The nearest town was too far from the quarry, so he built his family a house near the excavation site. Thanks to Mr. Carnegie's generosity, the Douglass's were well equipped for their long stay. Their ample supplies included not only material for the house, but also a cow and some chickens. After that, Douglass and his team built a road from his cabin to the fossil beds.

The amount of fossil material and the location of it provided a substantial challenge to the excavators. At first, the rubble from the excavations had to be hauled away by wagons pulled by a team of horses. After that, a railroad was brought to the site to take away the waste material. Their zeal at this wonderful find, along with the financial support from Carnegie, caused Douglass and his crew to work on into the winter, sometimes enduring temperatures as low as 30° F.

By and by, the huge dinosaur, *Apatosaurus*, was uncovered. It was basically a complete skeleton including 64 tail vertebrae. When reconstructed, the great creature was fifteen feet tall at the arch of the back! Before the *Apatosaurus* was totally removed, a second was found at the site and then a third was discovered. It was now obvious that Douglass had hit upon a dinosaur bonanza. His letters to the museum director reflected his jubilation. However, shortly after he and his team were well into the business of extracting these giant creatures from their sedimentary graveyards, a government act made it possible for the land in this vicinity to be opened to homesteading.

News of this new development brought immediate anxiety to both Holland and Douglass. They realized that at any time someone could lay claim to that land, and in so doing, they could legally move their family in and the dinosaur hunters out. Big strings had to be pulled at once! Efforts were made to gain rights to the land, but they were challenged. Finally, Holland was able to gain assistance from his friend, Charles D. Walcott, the former director of the U.S. Geological Survey. Walcott, in turn, was able to convince President Woodrow Wilson to designate the dinosaur site and the 80 acres surrounding it as Dinosaur National Monument in 1915.

Douglass and his workers were now able to work without interruption or fear of having the excavations closed down. They proceeded full steam ahead for 13 years. It was no longer seasonal work; instead, the teams labored at their task year round.

One dinosaur after another was removed from the surroundings.

The complexity of this enterprise is graphically illustrated in the various unique facets of the excavations. The layers containing the fossils had been disrupted from their originally horizontal position. They now lay at sharp angles which did not make excavating easy. The first job was to dig through the material until they reached the layer containing the fossils. This meant dumping small mountains of debris nearby. Dynamite, drills and crowbars were utilized to get to the fossil itself. Along the floor of the excavation site (more than 100 feet in length), the workers laid a set of rails which led to a nearby cliff. The waste material was loaded into small mining cars and then pushed down the tracks to be dumped over the cliff. Once they extracted the fossils from the layers of rock, the bones were preserved and protected for transportation by being wrapped in burlap soaked in flour paste.

Carefully, then, they proceeded to lower the bones by ropes to a skid. Mules dragged the loaded skid down from the uplift to the level land below. Here the material was crated and driven by the use of high wheeled wagons to the closest railroad, which was over 60 miles away. From there, they had to be loaded aboard the train and transported across America to the museum at Pittsburgh.

The tremendous dedication and labor of Douglass and his crews was well rewarded. By 1922, 446 crates of fossils had been transported to the Carnegie Museum. This represented about 700,000 lbs. of dinosaur material. Twenty of the skeletons were more or less complete and were subsequently mounted at the Carnegie Museum. Many partial skeletons were also obtained as well as many fragments. In all, thirteen separate dinosaur species were identified from remains found in this one great graveyard.

ROY CHAPMAN ANDREWS

The discovery of dinosaurs in Central Asia did not begin as a search for dinosaurs. Actually it began as an attempt to demonstrate that man had his beginnings in this area of the world. First, Henry Fairfield Osborn of the American Museum of Natural History and then, several years later, William D. Matthews, also proposed the idea that Central Asia was the place where man and the mammals had their origins.

Though not all scientists agreed with that opinion, there was one enterprising individual who thought it a fruitful suggestion. This was Roy Chapman Andrews who was on staff with the American Museum in New York. It was his idea to develop an expedition that would use both automobiles and camels for the work of traversing the wasteland of Mongolia in search of fossils. Recognizing the magnitude of the risk he was taking for both himself and the museum, Andrews pushed ahead with the idea.

Many specialists and technicians were carefully selected for the venture. This, in itself, was a challenging task, for they needed not only qualified individuals for the job, but also persons who would be able to get along harmoniously with each other under trying conditions. It was to be expected that many who were qualified would not want to leave a cozy position with a University in the States to risk their lives in the depths of Gobi desert.

Finally, the team was gathered. Its leader was Roy Chapman Andrews. Others of the expedition group included Walter Granger, the chief paleontologist and Geologists C.P. Berkey and Frederick Morris.

As the expedition trekked along en route to Ulan Bator, the capital of Mongolia, they came across many fossils, but they were not human. Instead they were mammalian and dinosaur fossils. They collected fossils here (Iren Dubasu), but could not stay for any in-depth probing. Finally they reached Ulan Bator.

After resting sufficiently there, they headed straightway into the vast Gobi. The direction was southwest. This was a part of the expedition which was primarily for the purpose of reconnaissance. After many weeks of explorations, they turned east toward the expeditions headquarters in Peking. After awhile, the trail they were following came to a great basin of sandstone where they made the momentous discovery of the now famous Flaming Cliffs. They were so named because of the way they appeared when the setting sun shone on the red rocks.

There, beneath this beautiful natural wonder, they found many fossils, not of mammals, but of dinosaurs. The dinosaurs, however, were not of a sort with which Walter Granger was familiar. Amidst the bones they also found fossilized eggshells, which some considered to have been laid by large birds. They designated this site Shabarakh Usa. Very little work would be done on the site, however, for it was necessary to press on to fulfill their reconnaissance and to also escape the desert before the harsh weather of winter set upon them.

The next year the expedition took to the fields with a readiness to make the most of the excavation sites previously discovered. More paleontologists were added to the team including Albert Johnson who had earlier worked with Barnum Brown in America.

Their first stop was at Iren Dubasu where they had first spotted the dinosaur fossils. Several quarries were developed there. They found the bones of both flesh eating and plant eating dinosaurs piled one upon another. This particular find is valuable for two special reasons: 1) it provided an excellent opportunity to obtain a variety of dinosaurs skeletons all in the same area, and 2) due to the configuration of the many dinosaurs one upon another, we were able to better appreciate the extent and intensity of the deluge which both killed and fossilized them.

After a most successful time of collecting these fossils, they proceeded westward to the colorful Flaming Cliffs. They arrived there in the very heart of Mongolia in July of 1923. For two seasons, they worked there--in 1923 and 1925.

By the end of these two highly profitable digs, they had obtained a fine collection of bones belonging to a new dinosaur which was given the name *Protoceratops*. The name, unfortunately, has nothing to do with the character of the dinosaur. The term "ceratops" identifies it with the horned dinosaur. The term "proto," however, is an attempt to force an evolutionary interpretation upon the particular dinosaurs they had found. *Protoceratops* had no horns, yet it had a body and skull design that included the neck shield of the other cerotopsians, such as *Triceratops*. *Protoceratops* was therefore interpreted to be an early form of the cerotopsians. Supposedly, it had taken hundreds of thousands of years for the horns to develop. Of course, there is no evidence of such a development. We refer the reader at this point to see our presentation of *Protoceratops* in the text for a more complete treatment of this problem.

Nevertheless, the success in dinosaur excavations at Flaming Cliffs was phenomenal. By the time they had finished, they had collected more than a hundred specimens of the new protoceratopsians.

Another factor which made this dig unparalleled was that they were able to find these particular dinosaurs in all stages of growth. They ranged from hatchlings all the way to fully grown adults. In addition to the dinosaur, other kinds of reptiles were also found at Shabarakh Usa, including alligators and a pond turtle. Many small mammal skulls were also found in this location.

These are typical of the kind we would expect to find in a land where many reptilian forms thrived. Today, one would not expect to find zebras or cows grazing near streams where alligators were to be found; however, in those same locations today such as the Amazon and Congo Rivers, you would find the small mammals. Such fossil evidence does not speak convincingly of an area where mammals were first evolving, but of an area where small mammals would be most likely to cohabit with the reptilian kind. In America, for instance, this even included the opossum. Fossilized skulls were found in Montana, proving that they lived during the days of the dinosaurs.

In the three years of excavation, (1922, 1923 and 1925) in outer Mongolia, the Asiatic expeditions had collected dinosaurs from a variety of sites. However, since their vehicles were not adequate for transporting the giant dinosaur skeletons, they had to leave most of the bones at the various sites. Nevertheless, more than 100 reptile and mammal skulls were returned as well as the remains of a small *Protoceratops*.

Each of the distinct locations were isolated basins, indicating the presence of large bodies of water. Such locations also indicate the expected destination or dumping grounds of the sediment bearing rivers of the great Flood. Once these rivers flowed into the quiescent water of the deeper basins, the velocity of the river would be greatly reduced, allowing the sediment to settle and begin to lithofy. The excellent preservation of so much fossil material demonstrates that this process must have been rapid.

Index